Freedom and Morality and Other Essays

Freedom and Morality and Other Essays

A. J. Ayer

CLARENDON PRESS · OXFORD

Oxford University Press, Walton Street, Oxford OX2 6DP

Oxford New York Toronto
Delhi Bombay Calcutta Madras Karachi
Petaling Jaya Singapore Hong Kong Tokyo
Nairobi Dar es Salaam Cape Town
Melbourne Auckland

and associated companies in
Beirut Berlin Ibadan Nicosia

Oxford is a trade mark of Oxford University Press

Published in the United States
by Oxford University Press, New York

© A. J. Ayer 1984

First published 1984
Reprinted 1985
Reprinted (new as paperback) 1986

Library of Congress Cataloging in Publication Data
Ayer, A. J. (Alfred Jules), 1910–
Freedom and morality and other essays.
Includes index.
1. Philosophy—Addresses, essays, lectures.
2. Liberty—Addresses, essays, lectures.   3. Ethics—
Addresses, essays, lectures.   I. Title.
B1618.A49A94 1984   192   83-26845
ISBN 0-19-824731-1
ISBN 0-19-824961-6 (Pbk.)

British Library Cataloguing in Publication Data
Ayer, A. J.
Freedom and Morality and other essays.
1. Philosophy
I. Title.
192   B1618.A94
ISBN 0-19-824731-1
ISBN 0-19-824961-6 (Pbk.)

Printed in Great Britain
at the University Printing House, Oxford
by David Stanford
Printer to the University

To Rosanne Richardson

Preface

The first three of the essays which compose this book are transcripts of the Whidden lectures, instituted in honour of Dr Howard P. Whidden, a former chancellor of McMaster University, and delivered by me at that university in Hamilton, Ontario, on 18–20 October 1983 under the overall title of 'Freedom and Morality'. They have not been previously published. Neither has the essay 'On Causal Priority' which I was stimulated to write by the late Mr. J. L. Mackie's book *The Cement of the Universe*, which was published by the Oxford University Press in 1971.

All the remaining essays have been previously published and are reprinted with only one or two minor corrections. 'The Causal Theory of Perception' was my contribution to a symposium with Mr L. J. Cohen at the Joint Session of the Mind Association and the Aristotelian Society. It was published in Supplementary Volume I.I of the *Proceedings of the Aristotelian Society* for 1977. 'On A Supposed Antinomy' was published in *Mind*, Vol. I.XXXII, N.S., No. 325, January 1973. I have since learned that a similar solution of the puzzle had already been propounded by Professor Ardon Lyon.

'Identity and Reference' first appeared in *Philosophia*, Philosophical Quarterly of Israel, Vol. 5, No. 3, in July 1975. It was reprinted in *Language in Focus*, a volume edited by A. Kasher in honour of Y. Bar Hillel and published by D. Reidel Publishing Company in 1976. Copyright © 1976 by D. Reidel Publishing Co., Dordrecht, Holland. 'Self-Evidence' was my contribution to a book of essays edited by E. Pivcević and called *Phenomenology and Philosophical Understanding*. It was published in 1975 by the Cambridge University Press.

The essay 'Wittgenstein on Certainty' is a transcript of a lecture delivered at the Royal Institute of Philosophy in 1973 and published by Macmillan in 1974 in a volume entitled *Understanding Wittgenstein*. 'An Honest Ghost?' was one of a collection of critical essays with an introduction by Gilbert Ryle, entitled *Ryle: A Collection of Critical*

Essays, edited by Oscar P. Wood and George Pitcher, copyright © 1970 by Doubleday and Company Inc., New York. Finally, the essay 'The Vienna Circle' is a version of a lecture delivered to a Wittgenstein Congress in Kirchberg, Austria, in 1981 and published by Springer-Verlag, Vienna, in 1982 in *Rationality and Science*, a volume commemorating the centenary of the birth of Moritz Schlick.

I wish to thank the editors, publishers, and institute in question for giving me permission to reprint these articles, as well as Linn Nolan and Susie Lance of the Provost's office at Dartmouth College for typing the hitherto unpublished essays, Mrs Guida Crowley for secretarial assistance which included typing the index and my wife for helping me to compile it.

26 November 1983   A. J. Ayer
51 York Street
London W1

Contents

1   *Freedom and Morality*

PART A: THE CONCEPT OF FREEDOM

The idea that men are free agents governs nearly all our assessments
of human conduct. It is a presupposition not only of moral and legal
judgements but also, as Sir Peter Strawson has pointed out,[1] of our
emotional attitude towards other people and towards ourselves. If
someone's behaviour fills me with gratitude or resentment, whether
on my own account or on behalf of others whom it affects, I am
assuming that the agent need not have acted as he did. If there are
occasions when my own actions awake in me a sense of pride or
remorse, I believe in either case that I could have avoided their
performance. I think that there is a tendency to underestimate the
very wide area over which this concept extends, although it is more
generally acknowledged that an agent must be deemed to have acted
freely if he is to be a candidate for moral disapproval or legal
punishment.

I think it clear that what confronts us here is a single concept and
not a family. The sense in which I must have acted freely in order to
deserve praise or blame, reward or punishment, for my action is the
same as that in which I must have acted freely in order to merit
gratitude or resentment on account of what I did, or to have the
right to feel pride, or reason to feel remorse. The point that we are
making use of the same concept is worth stressing, since those who
argue that people never deserve to be punished, perhaps on the
ground that, strictly speaking, no one can ever help behaving as he
does, might shrink from concluding, on the same ground, that our
feelings of gratitude or resentment have no legitimate objects, or that
one never has good reason to feel remorse or pride. Yet if the
argument abolishes freedom in the first type of case, it does so also in

---

[1] In his 'Freedom and Resentment' in his book of essays with that title.

the second. If we wish to differentiate between them, we have to acquiesce in being irrational.[2]

But is such an argument valid? What exactly is the concept of freedom which it might be thought to threaten? This is a question to which centuries of discussion have failed to bring a definitive answer. Perhaps the only point on which there is general agreement is that it is a necessary condition for a man to have acted freely that he could have acted otherwise. But what is meant by saying that an agent could have acted otherwise, whether this condition is ever fulfilled, whether it is sufficient as well as necessary, and what else is necessary if it is not sufficient, are all of them questions in dispute. A further complication is afforded by those who believe that the condition is not fulfilled, or at least that we are not in a position to assume that it is, but still wish to preserve the notion of responsibility at least to a degree that justifies the insitution of reward and punishment. They therefore take the uncommon course of severing the notion of responsibility from the concept of freedom which it is usually held to presuppose, and either discard the concept of freedom altogether, as being wholly idle, or else give it a sense of their own which ties it to the notion of responsibility. I shall touch on their views, when I have done my best to analyse the concept of freedom as I believe it to be more commonly understood.

The first question is what is meant by saying that an agent could have acted otherwise. In an article entitled 'Freedom and Necessity', which I first published in 1946 and reprinted in my *Philosophical Essays* in 1954, I suggested that 'To say that I could have acted otherwise is to say, first, that I should have acted otherwise if I had so chosen; secondly, that my action was voluntary, in the sense in which the actions, say, of a kleptomaniac are not; and thirdly, that nobody compelled me to choose as I did.'[3] And I added, correctly, that the satisfaction of these three conditions did not entail that my action could not be causally explained. Without wishing to withdraw this last point, I no longer think that my analysis was adequate. When I recently reread this passage I wondered what I had thought that the second condition added to the first, since I said of the kleptomaniac that 'Whatever he resolved to do he would steal all the same'.[4] I now see, however, that this does rather more than

---

[2] See my 'Freedom and Rationality' in *Philosophical Subjects. Essays presented to P. F. Strawson.*
[3] Op. cit., p. 282.   [4] Ibid., p. 280.

violate my first condition, since to deny that an agent would have acted differently if he had so chosen does not quite amount to denying that he would have acted differently, whether he had chosen to or not. The actions which this last proviso excludes from being voluntary are all those that occur independently of the agent's choice. Whether this adequately covers the example of the klepto-maniac is open to doubt. It might be argued that his trouble was not that his choosing not to steal was ineffective but rather that he could not bring himself to make that choice.

If this is correct, the example of the kleptomaniac seems rather to lead into my third condition than to expand the first. The point of my third condition was to find room for freedom of action within the embrace of determinism. Not that I took the thesis of determinism to have been conclusively established. If we conceive of human actions, not simply as physical movements, but also as involving mental antecedents, it seemed, and still seems to me an open question whether they are all fully susceptible of a causal explanation. To say that they could all be explained in causal terms if only we knew enough is an empty claim. In order to give it content we have to produce some theory of which we can actually make use to account for them; which means, among other things, that it does more than merely fit them into generalizations *ex post facto*; for given that no restrictions are placed on the type or complexity of the generaliz-ations, this will always be feasible. At present, we do not command any such theory, but we are also not in a position to prove that we never shall.

An argument has, indeed, been advanced, by Professor Donald Davidson,[5] which purports to prove, first, that mental events are anomalous, when conceived under mental descriptions, and secondly, that, as answering also to physical descriptions, they are subject to strict causal laws; but I believe that the argument is defective on both counts. The ground on which it is alleged that events conceived as answering to mental descriptions elude the grasp of strict laws is that we cannot pin-point the events; we cannot gain enough information from the subject's behaviour to be sufficiently sure that our descriptions are accurate. At the same time, it is assumed that we can pin-point these events with sufficient accuracy to be able to list them as causes and effects; for this is taken to imply that they are governed by strict causal laws, and this in its turn is taken to imply

[5] See his 'Mental Events' reprinted in his book *Essays on Actions and Events*.

that they answer to physical descriptions. No other evidence is offered. But in the first place it has not been shown that an event cannot have an accurate mental description, however hard this may be for outside observers to discover, and secondly the only evidence there can be that mental events are terms in causal relations is that they are associated under mental descriptions with other mental and physical events. Yet this in no way implies that they answer also to physical descriptions. If Davidson insists, in my view wrongly, that for an event to be a term in a particular causal relation it must fall under a strict causal law, the most that his argument achieves is to throw unmerited doubt on the assumption that mental events do play a causal role.

This is not to say that mental events, and consequently the actions to which some of them give rise, are not causally determined, under some description, but only that the proof is lacking one way or the other. The same applies, in my view, to the hypothesis that actions, regarded simply as bodily movements, are causally determined, though this is to raise a different issue from that which we have been discussing. If I do not dwell on it further, it is because I do not think that it is central to our enquiry. Whether we conceive of actions, in the narrowest possible way, as physical movements, or more widely, and in a more customary way, as including intentions, or more widely still as including both intentions and motives, the salient point is not that we can prove them to be causally determined but that we cannot prove them not to be so. That is the position with which a tenable theory of freedom has to come to terms.

This accounts for the formulation of my third condition in my 'Freedom and Necessity'. There had been considerable argument among philosophers over the issue of freedom and determinism. Some thought that freedom was excluded by the rule of causality; others went so far in the opposite direction as to hold that freedom presupposed determinism; others maintained that they pass each other by. I tried to take a middle position by making freedom consistent with some forms of causality but not with all. I argued that freedom was to be contrasted not with causality as such but only with those forms of causality that amounted to constraint.

But what were these? My answer took the form of giving examples, such as my being compelled by another person to do what he wanted, whether he had obtained total control over my will, for example by hypnotizing me, or had acquired an habitual ascendency over me, or put me in a position, say by holding a pistol at my head, in which no reasonable person would choose to disobey him. And it was to these examples that, rightly or wrongly, I assimilated that of the kleptomaniac. What it now seems to me that they have, or were thought to have, in common is that *either* the agent's choice is not a causal factor, as in the case of his being hypnotized or, as I construed it, in that of the kleptomaniac, *or* his power of choice is nullified, as by the threat of death or by his subservience to another's will. I should have added that it is not a case of all or nothing. Freedom is implied by responsibility, and responsibility is thought to be diminished by one's being under the influence of drink or drugs, or by one's suffering from some form of mental illness. The question may then be raised how far it was in one's power to avoid getting into these states. This is not an easy question and I know of no authoritative answer to it.

This is, indeed, a facet of a wider problem. I think that there is no doubt that we do have a concept of constraint which, although its boundaries are not sharply drawn, is anyhow narrower in its extension than the concept of causality. It appears to operate in two principal directions, either as limiting our power of translating our choices into action or as limiting our power of choice itself. So far we have concentrated on cases of the second type, but examples of the first come readily to mind. Only too often our freedom of action is restricted by the opposition of other persons, the hostility of our physical environment, or some lack of capacity, whether physical or mental, in ourselves. Here too there is some uncertainty at what point this lack of capacity is to be counted as constraint.

It is important to note the distinction between these two types of cases, because many philosophers, from John Locke onwards, have taken the view that it is only cases of the first type that affect the question of our freedom. They have been content to say that we act freely to the degree that we have the power to act as we choose. As Locke put it, 'So far as a man has power to think or not to think, to move or not to move, according to the preference or direction of his own mind, so far is a man *free*.'[6] At the same time, he, and others after him, have denied the possibility of our having a comparable freedom of choice. Indeed, Locke goes so far as to say that the question *Whether man's will be free or no* is unintelligible, his reason being that 'Liberty, which is but a power, belongs only to *agents*, and

[6] *Essay Concerning Human Understanding*, II, ch. XXI, sect. 8.

cannot be an attribute or modification of the will which is also but a power.'[7] As he explains later on, 'Powers are relations not agents: and that which has the power or not the power to operate, is that alone which is or is not free, and not the power itself. For freedom, or not freedom, can belong to nothing but what has or has not a power to act.'[8]

If Locke and his followers are right, the moralist who feels threatened by determinism need only explore the aftermath of our volitions. He has to make clear in what manner our actions issue from them, whether or not this is consistent with their being explicable in purely physical terms, whether, if they are so explicable, he can still find room for moral responsibility. The prevalent view is that he can still find a niche for freedom of action, though we may have to do a little tinkering with our ordinary notions of responsibility if they are to be accommodated as well. But is it altogether obvious that Locke and his party are right? It is all very well for Locke to write of the imbecility of attributing or denying powers to powers, but is there not another way of looking at the problem? If it is significant to ask whether a person could have acted otherwise, in a sense which carries the question whether he could have given effect to a different choice, is it not also significant to ask whether he could have chosen otherwise? If our moralist, enquiring into some particular action, were told that the agent could have done something else, if he had had a mind to, but that the answer to the question whether the agent could have chosen otherwise was that he could not or, worse still, that the question was nonsensical, should we expect him to conclude that the agent had acted freely?

I do not think that we should. A phenomenon which has given trouble to moral philosophers from Plato and Aristotle onwards, is that of incontinence, or weakness of will. How is it possible for an agent to judge that it would be better for him to do X than Y and still proceed to do Y? There is no doubt that this frequently happens, not only when the agent judges that X is a morally better action than Y but also when he judges that it is more conducive to his own interest. One may go so far as to say that he intentionally does Y, knowing all the time that he would rather do X, which is equally open to him. How can this be? I do not know the answer to this question, unless

---

[7] Ibid., sect. 14.   [8] Ibid., sect. 19.

we are going to be satisfied with saying that men are frequently irrational, but that is not my present concern. My reason for mentioning this problem is that it would not be seen as a problem at all unless it were believed that we can significantly be credited with freedom of choice. The incontinent man is not one who fails to carry out some action on which he has chosen to embark; he is one who chooses what he believes to be a worse course of action, when he believes that the choice of a better course of action is also open to him. For the purpose of my illustration, or indeed, for the presentation of the problem, it is not necessary that this second belief be true. It is sufficient that it be held.

This is not an isolated example. Many of our moral judgements bear on motives and they seem to imply that the agent, whose action is in question, had the power of choice. This is not to say that the motives themselves are supposed to be chosen, but rather that there are thought to be occasions on which an agent, being supplied with different motives, is free to choose the one from which he acts. Certainly, my examples in 'Freedom and Necessity' accorded with this approach. The man who was hypnotized was one deprived of the power of choice; the kleptomaniac was represented as one who had no option but to steal; the man with a pistol at his head had no reasonable alternative but to comply with his assailant's order; habitual subservience robbed one of any inclination to disobey. It will be remembered that these were offered as illustrations of constraint. The implication was that when the determining factors did not amount to constraint, the agent could fairly be accounted free not just to act in accordance with his choice but also to make one choice rather than another.

I wonder now if this distinction can bear the weight that I set upon it. I am not saying that we cannot lay down criteria for delimiting the cases in which we are subject to constraint. No doubt these criteria are rather rough, as they actually stand, but they could be sharpened if the need arose. The trouble is that, if we assume, for the sake of argument, that all our choices are causally determined, it is not clear how the nature of the causes can make so much difference; it is not as if the causes which do not come under the heading of constraint are any less efficacious than those that do. In my article, I argued that we should not be misled by talk of causal necessity; it came down to no more than the persistence of certain forms of association and why should we fuss over that? But now, I ask, what more is there to constraint? There is a type of person who under specifiable conditions addresses another in such a way that his victim falls into a trance; before bringing his victim out of the trance he instructs him to perform a certain action, let us say, something odd, like turning a somersault, at such and such a subsequent time; at the time indicated the victim performs the action. What is all this but a factual sequence of events which is capable of being generalized? The victim might have performed the same action, in order to amuse a friend, or to attract attention to himself, or test his suppleness, or for no special reason, just because he wanted to. In all these cases we should say that he could help himself, that he need not have done it. Why not in the other?

Well, one obvious difference is that in the case where he has been hypnotized, the victim has no choice. We are assuming that he turns a somersault, like an automaton, at the appointed time. If he were doing it to please a friend, his desire for this end would be a causal factor. In the case of the kleptomaniac, as we are conceiving it, the decision to steal does play a causal role. What he lacks is the power to choose otherwise. The man who is threatened with a pistol has this power in that it is open to him to defy his assailant, but we are assuming that it is a choice which it would not be reasonable for him to make.

But how can we say that our man has the option to defy his assailant if it is causally determined that he does not take it? We distinguished the man who turned the somersault to amuse his friend from the man who did it in obedience to a post-hypnotic suggestion, by the fact of his acting from a motive in a way that the other did not. But what difference does this make if his wanting to please his friend is itself the outcome of a causal sequence? The unkind answer is that he did act from a motive, however he came by it, which brings us back to Locke's position. But that is just what we are putting in question. We still need to show how we can sensibly talk of his being free to make some other choice.

Let us consider, then, what can be meant by saying of someone that he could have chosen otherwise. Or rather, let us take a step further back and return to the question what is meant by saying of someone who has performed a particular action that he could have acted otherwise. A suggestion, made by G. E. Moore, which I mentioned earlier as one that I followed in 'Freedom and Necessity', is that it means or at least entails that the agent would have acted otherwise, if he had so chosen. I no longer think that this entailment holds. Let us take a simple example. I used to be a heavy smoker of cigarettes but I have given them up. Consequently, I have not smoked a cigarette this morning. Even so I could have smoked one. Does this mean, or even imply, that I should have smoked one if I had so chosen? Not necessarily. It might well be the case that I had no immediate access to any cigarettes, and while I should have smoked one if it had been readily available, my desire was not strong enough to put me to the trouble of finding a tobacconist. If I had gone to the tobacconist, he might not have stocked the brand that I used to favour, or even any other brand that I could tolerate. This is not to say that I should have rejected all of his stock in any circumstances. No doubt my disinclination would have been overcome by a sufficiently heavy bribe. But by now we have come quite a long way from saying that I should have smoked a cigarette if I had so chosen. Nor does one save the situation by putting in a *ceteris paribus* clause, for '*ceteris paribus*' must here be taken to mean 'things otherwise being as they were' and the point is just that as things were I should *not* have smoked a cigarette, if I had so chosen, while it remains true that I could have smoked one. The most that can be maintained is that my not choosing was a necessary component of some set of conditions which were jointly sufficient for my abstinence, but this falls short of its being a sufficient condition on its own. We seem, therefore, obliged to conclude that 'I could have smoked a cigarette this morning' might be true in circumstances where 'I should have smoked a cigarette this morning if I had chosen to' was false, so that the entailment does not hold, let alone the suggested equivalence. What does hold is the converse entailment. If it were true that I should have smoked a cigarette if I had so chosen, then it follows that I could have smoked one.

The same considerations apply to the attempt, which Moore also made, to analyse 'I could have chosen otherwise' along similar lines. Suppose that I chose to spend my summer holidays in France. I can subsequently say that I could have chosen to spend them in Italy instead. This does not mean, or even entail, that I should have chosen to spend them in Italy if I had chosen so to choose. The phrase 'if I had chosen so to choose' is difficult to interpret but presumably it refers to my coming to some decision to make this choice. But then I might have had cause to go back on this decision; the friend with whom I had arranged to travel might have opted against Italy and I might not have cared enough one way or the other to insist upon my choice. So it would not be the case that I should have chosen to go to Italy if I had chosen so to choose. I did choose so to choose, yet I actually chose to go to France. Nevertheless it remains true that I could have chosen to go to Italy and true also that this follows from the proposition that I should have chosen to go to Italy if I had chosen so to choose. It is the converse that does not hold.

It might be thought that this approach led to a vicious regress 'I should have acted otherwise if I had so chosen'; 'I should have chosen otherwise if I had chosen so to choose'; 'I should have chosen to choose otherwise, if I had chosen so to choose to choose'; and so on. There seems, however, to be no compelling reason to carry this sequence beyond the second stage. The question: Was I free to choose to choose otherwise than as I did? has no clear meaning and the difficulty of attaching a meaning to each stage will increase as the sequence progresses. If I do not press this point, it is because we have already discovered a stronger ground for rejecting this type of analysis. For the same reason, I shall not enter into the question, debated by Austin, Davidson, and others, whether sentences like 'I can if I choose' do or do not express causal conditionals.

Instead, I am going to attack the whole problem from a different angle. What are the limitations upon an agent's freedom? What are our grounds for saying that it is not within his power to perform such and such an action? To begin with, we find it obvious that he cannot do what is logically impossible; if he tells us that he is searching for the largest prime number we can assure him that he is wasting his time. Neither do we credit him with the power to achieve what is physically impossible. He cannot travel faster than the speed of light. More interestingly, he is held unable to do what does not contradict the laws of nature as such, but is incompatible with the conjunction of what we take to be natural laws and the special circumstances of the agent. There are now a number of men in the world who are capable of running a mile in less than four minutes, but I am not one of them. My age, my lack of training, my physical condition make it impossible. Indeed, I can confidently say that it was impossible for me at any age. And what made it impossible was the fact that my not running at so great a speed was always deducible from a set of premises combining particular truths about my concurrent physical state with well-established anatomical hypotheses about the range of athletic accomplishments.

Examples of actions which are not ruled out by causal laws alone but by their conjunction with the circumstances of the agent are very common. As a general rule, I am free to go to Paris. There are aeroplanes, boats, and trains to take me there, and no impediment is placed in the way of my making use of them. Even so, I am not free to dine there this evening because it is already too late for any means of transport to get me there in time. We could complicate the example by supposing that I could get there in time if I could charter a private aeroplane. But I do not know how to set about doing this and if I did, it would cost me more than I could afford. But could I not run into debt? For me to do so for such a purpose would be quite out of character. No one who knows me well would expect me to. The set of particular and general statements which we are taking for granted do not go so far as to entail that I do not spend the money but they make it highly probable. This example is comparable to that of the man whose life is threatened. Our stock of knowledge about the situation and human character, and perhaps about his character in particular, does not entail that he complies with the demands of his assailant but makes it improbable that he refuses and, on a different scale of judgement, also makes it irrational.

This is a scale to which we often turn when we make judgements of what is or is not in our power. I say 'I am sorry, I cannot lend you the money' not because I do not have it but because it is nearly all I have and to lend it to you would be to take an unjustifiable risk, especially if you are the sort of person on whom I cannot count to pay it back. Moral considerations may also come into play. I say that I cannot dine with you on Tuesday, not because I am taking a set of propositions to be established from which it follows that I shall not, but because I already have an engagement for that evening and I make it a rule not to break previous engagements. Not that I follow the rule unconditionally. There are circumstances in which I do break it but they do not obtain in this instance. Perhaps they will come to obtain. My previous engagement may be cancelled or you may offer me so strong an inducement that I contrive to get out of it, with or without a feeling of guilt. If the governing considerations are moral, what is impossible at one time may become possible at another, or the reverse.

The same applies in the domain of fact. Fifty years ago no one was free to walk on the moon. The current physical theories, combined with all the particular statements which formed the corpus of our knowledge, collectively entailed that no one was performing this feat. Since then our premisses have changed. It remains true that I cannot walk upon the moon; I do not meet the conditions laid down for the participation in any programme of astronautical travel nor is there any prospect that, within my lifetime, excursions will be arranged in which my circumstances will allow me to participate. Probably this will be true of most people for some considerable time. Nevertheless, walking on the moon is something of which human beings have been found to be capable. The set of well-established propositions, both particular and general, from which it followed that no human being did so has turned out to have members not all of which are•true.

If this line of reasoning is correct, the emphasis falls upon the denial of freedom. The best way to make clear what is meant by saying that a person was free to perform a given action, whether he actually performed it or not, is to set out the conditions under which this power would not be granted to him. Evidently we do not admit of his doing what is generally forbidden by what we take to be the laws of logic or the laws of nature. It is not, indeed, very likely that anyone would claim such a power unless his purpose was to show that what we had taken to be a law of nature, or possibly even a law of logic, was not really so. The most common type of case is that in which a person's incapacity to perform a given action is proved by our adducing a set of antecedent circumstances from which in conjunction with some set of well-established general propositions it follows that the action is not done. Since the premisses which serve to exclude the action vary according to the circumstances of the agent we secure the truism that not everyone is equally free. An action which it is in the power of one person to perform may not be available to another, because of a difference in their physical or mental constitutions or in their spatio-temporal positions. This last factor is apt to be particularly important if the difference in the periods at which they live is also marked by an appreciable difference in what may be described as the common stock of knowledge.

We have already noted that we speak of incapacity in a weaker sense, when the conclusion that the action is not done is not entailed by the premisses but only rendered probable in some high degree, and in a still weaker sense, in which it runs counter to some moral principle which we consider it right or rational for the agent to adhere to. In an even weaker sense, the rule may be no more than a rule of taste or manners, 'You cannot prefer Landseer to Cézanne.' 'You cannot wear that tie with that suit.' Since such pronouncements make no claim to being literally true, they need not further concern us.

A great merit of the foregoing approach is that it covers not only freedom of action but freedom of choice. We are fully entitled to say that a person could not have chosen to perform a given action, if and only if we are in a position to adduce a set of circumstances, antecedent to the moment of choice, from which, in conjunction with some set of well-established hypotheses, it follows that the choice was not made. We may also admit the weaker senses in which the premisses make it improbable that the choice was made or the making of the choice runs counter to some moral, aesthetic, or social principle. Oddly enough, the choice of an action generally thought to be logically or physically impossible is not precluded, for there are people who seriously try to square the circle or emulate Superman. If we wish to avoid this consequence we must construe 'He chose to act in such and such a fashion' as entailing not merely that the action was seriously attempted but that it was actually performed. I suppose that either interpretation is sanctioned by ordinary usage.

The most interesting feature of our approach, and the one to which exception is most likely to be taken, is that freedom is made relative to what is or, to speak more strictly, what is thought to be our current state of knowledge. This is not to repudiate my earlier view that there need be no conflict between freedom and causality, so long as the causality is taken no further back than the operation of the agent's motive. I am quite content to treat motives as causes, partly because I do not require of a cause, especially in the field of human conduct, that it strictly determines its effect. What I mean by saying that the cause assigned to an action may not strictly determine it, is that the causal relation in this instance may rest on nothing stronger than a statement of tendency. As I put it in another context, 'For the most part, when we speak of the causes of human behaviour we use the word "cause" in the sense of "necessary condition". We are claiming that the behaviour in question would not have been forthcoming if such and such an event had not oc-curred. The idea behind this is that there is a finite number of ways in which such behaviour comes about. That is to say, the behaviour is linked with different events by different generalizations of tendency. If one of these generalizations is exemplified on a particular occasion, and the others not, we say that the event which enters into the generalization is the cause. So, I may judge that someone is angry because he has been insulted. To arrive at this conclusion, I need not believe that being insulted always makes him angry, or that nothing else does. It is enough that I believe the suffering of an insult to be one of the conditions under which people of his sort frequently become angry, and that I have no present evidence for any rival explanation. In general, this is the way in which motives operate.'[9]

In saying no more than this is, in general, the way in which motives operate, I am leaving room for the possibility of someone's adducing a set of conditions, the combination of which with a motive of a given sort is related to a subsequent form of action by a strict causal law. Evidently, these conditions would have to include the agent's possession of some appropriate beliefs. At the same time, as I have already said, I do not believe that any such laws are actually available. So long as they are not available, the motives which we rightly regard as the causes of the actions which they motivate will not fully determine them. The reason for this, as I have just explained, is that their causal power will rest on nothing stronger than statements of tendency. It might, therefore, be suggested that there was room here for the insertion of freedom. I doubt, however, if this is the proper place for it. Neither the fact that a given combination of desire and belief does not invariably result in the same intentional action, nor its converse, the fact that intentional action of a given sort does not invariably issue from the same combination of desire and belief, seems to me to contribute to the characterization of free agency. It is true that my theory ties freedom to ignorance and uncertainty but the tie is knotted at an earlier stage. The uncertainty is not manifested by any limitation of the agent's power to do what he chooses but consists rather in the fact that his choices fit very loosely into a causal framework, if they are explicable at all. To make the point more clearly, the fact that a person's actions are 'rationalized', as Davidson puts it,[10] by his desires and beliefs does not derogate from his freedom even though

---

[9] *Vide The Central Questions of Philosophy*, p. 180.
[10] See his 'Freedom to Act' reprinted in his *Essays on Actions and Events*.

motives are causes. What is required is that we should not be equally well equipped to treat the rationalizing elements as effects.

This does mark a departure from my earlier position. I do not in fact believe that we possess the information which would enable us to account for a person's desires and beliefs either in terms of psychological, or of psychophysical, or of purely physical laws. Neither do I think that we are at all likely to obtain it, at least in the foreseeable future. Nevertheless, as I said earlier, I do not think that the possibility can be excluded *a priori*, and if it were realized then my present theory would commit me to denying us the possession of freedom of choice.

The awkward question is how much this would matter. We could still fall back upon the Lockean conception of a free agent as one who is not prevented from doing what he chooses and it might well be thought that a freedom which was relative to our state of knowledge was not worth very much. The obstacle to this way of thinking would be that, under our present system of concepts, freedom of choice is implied by the ascription of responsibility, and we surely do not want to give this up. Even if we were able to dissociate reward and punishment from any notion of desert and justify them only by their effects, we could not deal so lightly with what Strawson has called our reactive attitudes. I doubt if we could abandon them and even if we could, it would not be desirable. Our lives would be impoverished rather than enriched, if we could find no use for such concepts as those of pride and gratitude. Yet they too presuppose the ascription of responsibility and consequently freedom of choice.

But why can we not be content just to let things be? Since we do not possess the knowledge which alone could put us in a position to prove that an agent could not have chosen otherwise, we are entitled to grant him freedom of choice. Having granted him freedom of choice, we could happily continue to regard him as a moral agent and make him the subject and object of reactive attitudes.

The word that may give us pause here is 'happily'. I am persuaded that we do in fact take ascription of responsibility to imply freedom of choice, but if my account of freedom is correct, it is hard to see why we should. Why should the fact that we are unable to explain a person's choices in causal terms make him responsible for them in a way in which he would not be responsible for choices for which we did have, or thought we had, a causal explanation? In the cases where we lack a causal explanation and despair of finding one, we may suspect the presence of chance. Why should this be regarded as furnishing a basis for the ascription of responsibility?

An obvious conclusion to draw is that the concept of freedom which is here in question is not the one that I have analysed. But what alternative is there? I strongly suspect that we have unearthed a confusion in current thought and that, perhaps as a legacy of theology, we imply what Jonathan Bennett has rightly called 'A logically unsatisfiable concept of accountability – one which will not let a person count as blameworthy unless he is "free" or "autonomous" or "self-made" in a sense in which it is logically impossible to be free or autonomous or self-made.'[11] If this is true we are not left without resource. We can fall back on Locke's conception of freedom and modify our concept of responsibility so that it implies freedom of action rather than freedom of choice. What we may have to sacrifice, or very greatly modify, is our concept of desert.

[11] See his 'Accountability' in *Philosophical Subjects. Essays presented to P. F. Strawson*, p. 26.

PART B: ARE THERE OBJECTIVE VALUES?

Nearly fifty years ago, in a chapter boldly entitled 'Critique of Ethics and Theology', which was included in my first book, *Language, Truth and Logic*, I remarked that the strictly ethical contents of what I called 'the ordinary system of ethics' were divisible into four groups. These were said to be 'first of all, propositions which express definitions of ethical terms, or judgements about the legitimacy or possibility of certain definitions'; secondly, 'propositions describing the phenomena of moral experience and their causes'; thirdly, 'exhortations to moral virtue'; and lastly, 'actual ethical judgements'.[12] I criticized 'ethical philosophers' for their failure to observe these distinctions and then declared it 'easy to see that only the first of our four classes, namely that which comprises the propositions relating to the definitions of ethical terms, can be said to constitute ethical philosophy'.

Propositions describing the phenomena of moral experience and their causes were handed over to the sciences of psychology or sociology. Exhortations to moral virtue were simply denied the status of propositions, and accordingly excluded from both philosophy and science. As for 'the expressions of ethical judgments', which remained to be characterized, they succumbed to a governing principle of the book, that philosophy was confined to the activity of analysis, consisting at best in the provision of definitions, with the result that I was able to disown them also. 'A strictly philosophical treatise on ethics should', I said, 'make no ethical pronouncements, but it should, by giving an analysis of ethical terms, show what is the category to which all such pronouncements belong.'[13]

Looking back on this passage, I find it not so much mistaken as unduly scholastic. The distinctions that I made were valid, but my use of them to lay fetters upon moral philosophy impoverished the subject to an unreasonable extent. For example, it is no doubt true that the question how we come to judge that certain types of conduct are morally commendable and others not is one for empirical investigation, but that it is not a reason why philosophers like Hutcheson and Hume, who found moral judgements upon moral

[12] *Language, Truth and Logic*, 1st edn., p. 150.
[13] Ibid., p. 151.

sentiments, should be debarred from trying to answer it. If one were wholeheartedly committed to the conception of philosophy as analysis, one might say that they were straying outside philosophy, but what would be the harm in that? Alternatively, one might conclude that ethics was not a purely philosophical subject. This could be a nuisance to librarians, but need not impede the moralist; so long as he talked sense, there would be no reason why he should tailor his enquiries to their convenience.

The distinction between the making of ethical pronouncements and ethical philosophy, as I defined it, is also one that is likely to be overstepped. It is now more familiarly known as the distinction between ethics and meta-ethics, or sometimes as that between ethical judgements of the first and second orders. The reason why it is likely to be overstepped is that there is a sense in which meta-ethical or second-order ethical judgements are answerable to those of the first order. A theory of what we are doing when we make ethical judgements must at least be consistent with the ethical judgements that the proponent of the theory is prepared to make. Thus if someone were to agree with G. E. Moore that the word 'good' stood for an indefinable non-natural quality, and that what was meant by calling an action right was that it produced, or was likely to produce, the greatest feasible quantity of good, then he could not consistently think it right to try to maximize his own welfare at the cost of what would appear to be a greater good to some other person. Similarly, if someone took the view that calling something good meant no more than that it was productive of pleasure, he could not consistently characterize pleasures of any one sort as better or worse than those of any other.

We must, however, be careful not to carry this point too far. There is no one-to-one correspondence between judgements of the two different orders. A hedonist is not bound to hold the meta-ethical theory that goodness is equivalent to pleasure. He can agree with Moore that good is indefinable and still maintain, as a synthetic judgement, that pleasure alone is good. The same conclusion can be reached by someone who takes the second-order view that ethical judgements are subjective, in a way that allows him to advocate hedonism as an ethical policy. This leaves it open whether the policy is one that he can consistently adhere to, but then the discussion moves to a different level. It is no longer a matter of there being any lack of harmony between one's theory of the status of moral principles and their actual content, but rather the more practical question whether these principles themselves can stand the test of particular instances. A man who professes himself a hedonist may be confronted with actual or imaginary examples of indulgences in pleasure of which he does not morally approve.

It is to the second question that writers about morals have paid the greater attention, just because the mere delimitation of the status of moral judgements is so largely neutral with respect to moral judgements of the first order; and an interest in morals is the more likely to be fostered, if not by the desire to elaborate a moral system, at least by the need to resolve particular moral issues. Here again the question whether those who pursue such enquiries are over-stepping the boundaries of philosophy is not of major consequence. If their reasoning is cogent, that should be enough.

In saying this, I do not wish to blur the distinction between first- and second-order theories of morality. Neither am I implying that the distinction can be assimilated to that which obtains between first- and second-order theories in other fields. The parallel holds, in so far as there is as little warrant for forbidding, say, the philosopher of mathematics from trespassing into mathematics as there is for confining the moral philosopher strictly to meta-ethics, but it breaks down in the way that the distinctions operate. The philosopher of mathematics, like the philosopher of physics, or the philosopher of law, is presented with an accepted body of doctrine, or at least a fairly definite quantity of material, which he is required to analyse or evaluate. The moral philosopher is not in a similar position. The reason is that morality of the first order is not a special subject like the others we have mentioned. A moralist may have indeed thought more deeply about moral questions than men ordinarily do; he is likely to have made a closer and more critical study of the varieties of moral theory. Even so, there remains a sense in which one cannot be learned in morals, in the way one can be learned in mathematics or learned in the law. First-order moral judgements are not the product of any special expertise.

But is this not to beg the question against those who hold that values are objective? It is, only in so far as it rules out two types of meta-ethical theory. One is the theory of Plato, according to which reality consists in a world of forms, which are dominated or organized by something called the form of the good. Knowledge of this form is available only to those who have undergone a special course of intellectual training in which it would appear that the study of mathematics plays a conspicuous part. Once they have grasped it, they obtain an insight into the nature of things, including human nature, which furnishes them with the answer to the question how men ought to live.

My reason for ruling out this theory is frankly that I do not understand it. I do not know what the form of the good can be unless it be the common quality of goodness, and I do not see why the conception of this quality should be thought especially difficult to acquire, or what a training in mathematics has to do with it. It is noteworthy that when Plato discusses moral questions, as he does in the early Socratic dialogues, the arguments with which he furnishes Socrates do not rely on any recondite source of understanding, and that when, in a late dialogue, the *Philebus*, he tries to establish a hierarchy of goods, assigning for instance a higher rating to knowledge than to pleasure, the notion of anyone possessing a specialized acquaintance with the form of the good plays no part in the argument.

The other type of theory which has been ruled out is that in which the correct principles of conduct, or assessments of value, are supposed to be revealed by some oracle or deity, either directly to anyone who approaches them in the proper fashion, or to some specially qualified devotees who then make their views more generally known. The objection here is not just that there is no good reason to believe in the existence of any such oracle or deity, but rather that no set of moral principles or values can be founded on authority. The point, already made by Plato in his dialogue *Euthyphro*, and by many philosophers after him, is that the claim that Zeus, or for that matter any other god, is good, or that what he commands is right, is emptied of any content, beyond the mere assertion of the deity's existence, if his nature is made the criterion of goodness or his wishes the criterion of what is right. For our claim then becomes the mere tautology that God is what he is or that he wills what he wills. It is consistent with his being what, by our ordinary standards, we should consider a wicked tyrant. Thus, even theists who praise God for his goodness must be applying an independent standard of morality. Their belief that their deity sustains this standard may provide them with a motive for adhering to it, but that is another question.

To show that judgements of value cannot be founded on authority is to take a step towards the conclusion that ethics is autonomous, but it does not go the full distance. There remains the possibility that moral principles, or particular moral judgements, are based on empirical matters of fact. For instance, if it were accepted that right actions were those that produced or were likely to produce a greater balance of pleasure over pain than any others that were feasible in the circumstances, it would be a question of fact what they were, though admittedly a fact that it would be very difficult to ascertain. Again, if it were accepted that to call something good was equivalent to saying that the speaker approved of it, or that it met with general approval in the society to which the speaker belonged, the assignment of value would be a straightforward empirical question. The same would apply if judgements of value were treated as the deliverances of a moral sense.

One thing which has militated against the acceptance of all theories of this kind is that they have been thought to fall foul of what G. E. Moore called the naturalistic fallacy. Let us take the suggestion that good is to be defined as what meets with general approval. The objection which Moore raised in *Principia Ethica* was that if this were correct, it would amount to the tautology that what meets with general approval meets with general approval, which is hardly a contribution to ethics; and he argued that the same would apply to the equation of good with pleasure or any other natural feature.

What Moore strangely failed to notice is that his argument does not apply only to the attempt to define a moral term like 'goods'. The same trick can be played with any definition at all. If the definition is accurate, the substitution within it of the defining expression for the one defined will always yield a tautology. For instance, to use one of Moore's own favourite examples, there is no question but that brothers are male siblings. If we make our substitution accordingly, we come out with the triviality that brothers are brothers. There is no fallacy here, but only an illustration of what has come to be known as the paradox of analysis. I have no solution of the paradox to offer, beyond remarking that although the definition is not itself a statement about words, as is proved by the fact that it could be equally well expressed in other languages, nevertheless it is only the linguistic information which it incidentally provides that makes it informative. What concerns us here is that the paradox does not inhibit definition whether of moral terms or any others.

Moore does, however, have a further argument which is specifically directed against any attempt to treat the term 'good' as complex and definable. The argument, as he states it, is that 'Whatever definition be offered, it may be always asked with significance, of the complex so defined, whether it is itself good.'[14] We may note at once that the argument does not appear destructive of attempts to define 'good' in other ethical terms. If someone were to suggest that 'being good in itself' was equivalent to 'being valuable for its own sake' then in raising the question whether what was valuable for its own sake was good in itself, one would most probably be understood as querying the accuracy of the definition, but our ability to frame this question would not automatically show the definition to be incorrect. On the other hand, if we revert to the suggestion that 'good' means being generally approved of, then to ask whether what is generally approved of is good could reasonably be construed not just as querying the accuracy of the definition but as raising a significant moral question, in which case we should have conceded that the definition was faulty. The difference would consist in the fact that in the second case we should be stripping the term 'good' of its normative force. To say that something is generally approved of is consistent with denying that one should prize it oneself. One is not committed to sharing the popular view.

If this is correct, what remains of Moore's naturalistic fallacy is no more than Hume's well-known contention that 'ought' is not derivable from 'is'. I believe this contention to be substantially correct, though it is exposed to technical counterexamples such as the proposition that if *A* is a policeman, then *A* ought to do whatever a policeman ought to do, or that if *A* is the same person as *B*, *A* and *B* have the same duties. A less trivial instance which has been thought to tell against it is drawn from the example of promising. It is claimed that from the purely 'is' statement that, under specifiable conditions, a man utters a sentence of the form 'I promise to do *X*', it logically follows that, other things being equal, he ought to do *X*. But the argument is invalid. It depends on the presupposition that we are placed within a moral climate in which it is an accepted principle that the utterance of certain words, under given conditions, constitutes

[14] See *Principia Ethica*, p. 15.

the assumption of a moral commitment. Not only that, but even when this assumption is made, in order to secure our normative conclusion, we need the further normative premisses that this moral climate ought to command our favour; in this particular instance, the extra premiss is that the institution of promising merits our allegiance.

I believe that this example is truly typical in that it will always be possible to discover, in cases where purely factual premisses appear to yield a definite normative conclusion, that a normative premiss has been tacitly assumed. This may, indeed, seem to be yet another case of begging the question since it is taken for granted that ethical statements are not purely factual. If the word 'purely' is understood to imply non-ethical, then surely the dice are loaded. It is hardly to be expected that a set of non-ethical statements will yield a particular ethical conclusion. Nevertheless there is an underlying issue. The question is whether a distinction between the descriptive and the normative, or, if you like, between fact and value can be reasonably sustained.

This question is complicated by the fact that the distinction is not clearly marked in ordinary usage. This applies even to the use of the term 'good'. According to the first of the headings under which it is listed in the *Shorter Oxford English Dictionary*, it is 'a term of general or indefinite commendation', but I suspect that it is most commonly used in a way that is captured by the fourth heading, 'useful, reliable for a purpose, efficient in a function, pursuit, creed, etc. (either specified or understood)'. In short, what is good, in this usage, is what comes up to standard, the standards themselves differing according to the nature of the activity which is being assessed. Very often, perhaps more often than not, the note of commendation is also sounded, as when we speak of a good scholar, a good drawing, or a good friend, but this is not always so. The implied verdict may be neutral, or it may go the other way. To speak of someone's making a good profit leaves it open whether one approves or disapproves of the financial transaction. A good liar is one who is successful in getting others to believe his falsehoods, a good hater one who nurtures his grievances. Most people would judge that bad liars and bad haters are more to be commended. One might expect 'a good forger' to be on a par with 'a good liar'. But, oddly enough, while forging itself is not endorsed, a good forger is apt to be more highly esteemed than a bad one. The reason for this is presumably that he displays greater skill. If greater skill in lying is not given similar credit, it is probably because it poses a greater social threat.

The example of the good forger is of interest because the moral implication is carried not by the ostensibly normative epithet, but by the descriptive noun. There are, in fact, a great many nouns and still more adjectives in which the two functions are combined. To call a man generous or courageous is both to describe and commend a feature of his character; to call him mean or cowardly is both to describe and condemn one. In some cases, the normative aura determines the choice of the descriptive term. For instance, the application of the term 'murderer' to those who kill is reserved for those instances in which the killing is held to be unjustified. In other cases, the tone or the circumstances in which it is uttered can give what appears to be a uniquely descriptive expression some normative tinge. In certain contexts, the sentence 'The window has been left open' can have the form of a reproach.

These remarks are commonplace. They would be of greater interest if they served to show that the descriptive and normative uses of language were inextricably entangled, but this seems not to be so. 'Cruel', for example, is an adjective of condemnation. It remains open to us to redescribe what we are condemning by using some such expression as 'taking pleasure in inflicting pain'. This is not to deny that the spectacle or even the thought of what is so described may itself produce a hostile reaction. The point is that the registering of the effect can in such a case be separated from the description of the cause. And I believe that such a process of neutralization is always feasible, whatever form the reaction to the neutral description takes.

Let us assume that this is so. We still have to answer the question how ethical terms and statements are to be regarded. In drawing the distinction between the descriptive and normative uses of language, I have not meant to rule out the theory that what we count as ethical statements are made true by natural facts. It would surely be a mistake to deny that such statements carried any normative force, but it might be that the attribution of certain natural qualities was always accompanied by a prescriptive component, even though the two were separable. In such a case, ethical statements would form a subclass of descriptive statements and it would need to be shown what specially distinguished them.

Another way in which ethical statements might be accounted true or false would be through their having components which stood for objective values. I am using the term 'objective value' in the way I think it is ordinarily understood, as representing what Moore called a non-natural quality. Thus, in my usage, the distinction between subjective and objective would cut across the distinction between cognitive and non-cognitive theories about morals. A theory which equated 'good' with 'being desired' or 'right' with 'being generally approved of' would be cognitive in so far as it would represent ethical statements as statements of fact, but also subjective in that the facts would be facts about human attitudes or feelings. The same would apply to the theory which equates moral judgements with the verdicts issuing from an alleged moral sense. The case of a utilitarian meta-ethics is more dubious. It seems reasonable to describe the question whether one or other course of action will produce the greater quantity of happiness as turning on an objective matter of fact. But the posing of human happiness as the proper end of action causes it to be ranked with subjective theories. If this is found objectionable, the same purpose can be served by dividing objective theories into two classes, those that are naturalistic and those that are not.

At the time when I wrote *Language, Truth and Logic*, I had not yet come to doubt whether Moore was right about his naturalistic fallacy, and it was on this ground that I rejected the only two naturalistic theories I thought worth considering, namely those that consisted in a subjectivist or in a utilitarian analysis of ethical terms. My argument was that 'it is not self-contradictory to assert that some actions which are generally approved of are not right, or that some things which are generally approved of are not good', and as against 'the alternative subjectivist view that a man who asserts that a certain action is right, or that a certain thing is good, is saying that he himself approves of it', I maintained that 'a man who confessed that he sometimes approved of what was bad or wrong would not be contradicting himself'. In the same way, I maintained that 'it is not self-contradictory to say that it is sometimes wrong to perform the action which would actually or probably cause the greatest happiness, or the greatest balance of pleasure over pain, or of satisfied over unsatisfied desire' and further 'that it is not self-contradictory to say that some pleasant things are not good, or that some bad things are desired'.[15]

[15] *Language, Truth and Logic*, 1st edn., pp. 153–4.

I gave no arguments in support of these assertions, but simply followed Moore's example in trusting my ear for ordinary usage. I still think that it did not lead me astray except perhaps in one instance. It is now not entirely clear to me that a man who said that he approved of what was wrong would not be contradicting himself. He plainly would not be if he were using the word 'wrong' in a descriptive sense as referring to the violation of some set of moral standards, which it would be open to him not to accept; but the context indicates that I intended his use of the word to be understood as evaluative, and surely when the word is so understood, and also when it is granted, as it was meant to be, that the approval in question was moral approval, there would be a logical contradiction in claiming to approve of what was wrong. I am inclined to agree, but still feel some hesitation. I am not fully persuaded that when Milton represents Satan as saying 'Evil be Thou my good' he is not making him voice a coherent moral policy; and one that consists in the violation of principles that Satan himself acknowledges. Diabolism would be a much tamer exercise if it consisted merely in violating a moral code which one did not share. It might be argued that Satan's is not a moral policy since it cannot be universalized. If evil consists, even partly, in suffering, he could not coherently wish that it be inflicted on himself. But even if the premiss of this argument is sound, which could be disputed, I do not find it obvious that the choice of oneself as a victim of diabolism is psychologically impossible.

However this may be, there are other grounds for rejecting the view that in declaring an action to be good or bad, right or wrong, one is actually stating that one approves or disapproves of it. For one thing, it commits us to holding that the expression of any moral judgement logically entails the assertion of one's own existence, and this does not seem plausible. If I sincerely say that it was wrong for Brutus to assist in killing Caesar, or that John Stuart Mill was a good man, I am, of course, expressing my own belief, as I do when I voice any honest judgement, whether of value or fact, but I am not making an assertion *about* myself. It is logically compatible with the content of these moral judgements, as distinct from the fact of my asserting them, that I should not exist.

Incidentally, the same objection holds against the view that in making a favourable moral judgement, for instance about an action, one is stating that it meets with the approval or disapproval of some set of persons, whether it be the majority of the members of one's own society or some other group. Here again, the point is that from the content of the judgement, it does not logically follow that any such group exists.

Another argument which has been thought to refute the type of subjectivism in which moral judgements are equated with statements about their authors' feelings, is that it rules out the possibility of any formal expression of moral disagreement. To return to one of our examples, if I were to say that Brutus was wrong in helping to kill Caesar, and someone else were to say that he was right, we should not, on this subjectivist view, be contradicting one another. He would be saying that he approved of Brutus's action and that I should be saying that I didn't and both of us would be speaking the truth. But do we not thereby arrive at the contradiction that Brutus's action was both right and wrong?

The answer is that we do not, though many philosophers, including at one time Moore, have supposed that we do. The reason why we do not is that we are making the meaning of the judgement change according to its author. 'Wrong' in *A*'s mouth is to mean 'disapproved of by *A*' and 'right' in *B*'s mouth is to mean 'approved of by *B*', and if *A* and *B* are different persons, these predicates are not incompatible. Indeed, the fact that they are not incompatible may itself be seen as an objection to this analysis. For if one person says that a particular action is wrong, and another that the same action is right, is it not obvious that they are contradicting one another?

Not, I think, entirely. What is obvious is that they disagree with one another, but there are more ways of disagreeing than by making mutually contradictory statements. For instance, if one person likes oysters and another dislikes them, they may express their disagreement by saying respectively that oysters are good to eat and that they are not, but here the appearance of formal contradiction is deceptive. It is not even strictly implied that the oysters taste differently to them, but only that one enjoys their taste and that the other does not. In such a case, also, it may be more accurate to describe them as giving expression to their disagreement rather than as making conflicting statements about themselves. Now may it not be the case that ethical dissent conforms to this pattern, when the natural features of the situation are not in dispute and the question at issue is not whether a commonly acknowledged standard is being satisfied? Could not the disagreement about the rightness or wrongness of Brutus's action be held to consist rather in the expression of conflicting attitudes than in the assertion of incompatible statements? Just as in the example of the oysters, the bestowal on the action by the opposing parties of what appear to be incompatible predicates would be logically deceptive.

Such, indeed, was the conclusion at which I arrived in *Language, Truth and Logic*. Having been led, perhaps through too docile an agreement with Moore over the naturalistic fallacy, to share his view that ethical concepts did not mark out any natural properties, and having excluded the possibility of their being satisfied by non-natural properties as being wholly unverifiable, I concluded that they were, as I crudely put it, 'mere pseudo-concepts'. What I meant by this, I went on to explain, was that 'the presence of an ethical symbol in a proposition adds nothing to its factual content'. I compared the semantic role played in a sentence by purely ethical predicates to the addition of special exclamation marks or the utterance of the sentence in a peculiar tone. The point I was making, as I then put it, was that 'the tone, or the exclamation mark, adds nothing to the literal meaning of the sentence. It merely serves to show that it is attended by certain feelings in the speaker.'[16] Consistently, I drew the conclusion that persons who voiced a fundamental disagreement over some moral question were not in formal contradiction. Each was expressing his own moral sentiments and the expression of conflicting feelings should not be confused with the making of incompatible statements. I added that ethical terms served not only to express feeling but also to arouse it, and so to stimulate action, being sometimes used in such a way as to give the sentences in which they occurred the force of commands, and I went on to suggest that 'we may define the meaning of the various ethical words in terms both of the different feelings they are ordinarily taken to express, and also the different responses which they are calculated to provoke.'[17]

This was one of the earliest attempts to develop in any detail what came to be known as the emotive theory of ethics. I say 'to develop in any detail' because the theory had already been suggested by C. K. Ogden and I. A. Richards in their book *The Meaning of Meaning*, of which the first edition appeared as early as 1923. It was

---

[16] Ibid., p. 158.   [17] Ibid., pp. 160–1.

from them that I borrowed the word 'emotive' which they used to cover all aspects of language other than what they termed the referential or symbolic. So far as the study of emotive language went, they were chiefly interested in its application to aesthetics, but they also claimed that when the word 'good' was used, as it had been by Moore in his *Principia Ethica*, as the name of an indefinable quality, its use was purely emotive. They admitted in a footnote that 'if we define "the good" as "that of which we approve of approving" or give any such definition when we say "this is good", we shall be making an assertion'.[18] It is only on an interpretation like Moore's that 'the word stands for nothing whatsoever and has no symbolic function'. The authors contrast this use of 'good' with that of a predicate like 'red'. 'When we say "this is red", the addition of "is red" to "this" does symbolize an extension of our reference, namely to some other red thing. But "is good" has no comparable *symbolic* function; it serves only as an emotive sign expressing our attitude to *this*, and perhaps evoking similar attitudes in other persons, or inciting them to actions of one kind or another.'[19] I must confess that I had read *The Meaning of Meaning* some years before I wrote *Language, Truth and Logic*, but I believe that my plagiarism was unconscious. If I had realized how closely I was following in the footsteps of Ogden and Richards, I think it very unlikely that I should not have acknowledged my debt to them.

One obvious objection to the emotive theory is that moral epithets do not occur only in simple indicative sentences like 'This is good.' We often say such things as 'If he did that, he acted rightly' or 'He would have been a better man if he had had a stricter upbringing', and we also allow inferences of the form, if *A* is worse than *B*, and *B* is worse than *C*, then *A* is worse than *C*. If, as Ogden and Richards put it, the ethical words stand for nothing whatsoever and have no symbolic function, it is difficult to see how they can figure in conditional sentences or sustain deductive inferences in the ways that our examples seem to illustrate.

I think that this objection is less formidable than it may appear at first sight. Once it is admitted, as in the case of 'this is good', that an emotive expression can be put into an assertoric form, there seems no sufficient reason why the disguise should not be adapted to cover one's emotive reaction to hypothetical instances. As for the

---

[18] *The Meaning of Meaning*, p. 125. [19] Ibid.

deductive inference, it has, indeed, to be assumed that our attitudes are consistent, but thereafter the inference is simply secured by the transitivity of the comparative form. Thus, on the same assumption, we can reason with equal validity, that if oysters are nicer than mussels and mussels are nicer than clams, then oysters are nicer than clams, but we are not thereby forced to conclude that the use of a word like 'nice' in such context amounts to more than the expression of the speaker's taste.

There is, however, something to be said for devising an assertoric form which could be adapted to the use of emotive expressions in conditional contexts and apparently deductive reasoning. Suppose that we render 'This is good' as 'This is to be approved of', where 'is to be' is construed in a purely prescriptive fashion. Then we can rewrite our examples, admittedly in somewhat clumsy English, as 'If he did that, he is to be approved of'; 'He would be more to be approved of if he had been more strictly brought up'; and more straightforwardly 'If A is more to be approved of than B, and B more than C, then A is more to be approved of than C.' This device has the advantage of locating the emotive reaction in the present, whatever the dating of its 'object' and whether the object is actual or hypothetical, and it also has the advantage of bringing out the prescriptive element in our use of ethical terms.

A more serious objection, perhaps, is that the emotive theory of ethics was put forward as an account of the way in which ethical terms are ordinarily used, in cases where their use is not merely descriptive of the success or failure of whatever is in question to satisfy some acknowledged standard, and that most people do not believe that when they make moral judgements of the kind envisaged by the emotive theory, they are merely expressing their moral sentiments and encouraging others to share them. What most people believe, it is alleged, is that such judgements are genuinely assertoric. They are ascriptions of absolute values. If true, they are made true by objective ethical facts.

So far as I know, this allegation is not the result of any systematic piece of social research. Neither, for that matter, was the emotive theory. Speaking only for myself, I was led to it by assuming first that we had a use for ethical terms, which was distinct from their relation to some accepted standard; secondly, for the reasons I have explained, that their use was not captured by any naturalistic theory; and, thirdly, that it was captured by the emotive theory, which had the advantage of being consistent with my general philosophical position. I was satisfied if the theory fitted the circumstances in which ethical terms were actually used, when they were employed in what might be called an absolute fashion. Whether most people believed that their linguistic habits conformed to my theory was a question that did not greatly trouble me. Naturally, I hoped to convince those who were of a philosophical frame of mind. But, as a question of second- rather than first-order ethics, it seemed to me to be one about which those who did not subject it to what I considered to be the right sort of philosophical analysis might easily be mistaken.

While I should still not allow common sense to be the judge concerning the merits of second-order theory, whether in ethics or in any other domain, I now think that it may be of interest to take into account what people believe that they mean, even though it may not lead one to change one's own account of the best interpretation to put upon their utterances, and I am also prepared to admit, for the sake of argument, and on the basis of casual observation, that when they use ethical terms in what I have called an absolute fashion many people do believe that they are reporting objective ethical facts.

My main reason for making this admission is that I wish to discuss what has come to be known as the 'error theory' of morals. This is the theory put forward by J. L. Mackie in one of his later books, *Ethics*, which was published in 1977. The first sentence of the first chapter is 'There are no objective values.' Mackie explains a little later on that his thesis, which he calls moral scepticism, is an 'ontological thesis, not a linguistic or conceptual one'.[20] Whether or not people who make ethical judgements believe themselves to be referring to objective values, and whether or not moral philosophers give an account of moral judgements which implies that they do have such a reference, the fact remains that there are no such things. They do not form part of what Russell called the ultimate furniture of the world.

Though Mackie denies that he is putting forward a linguistic or conceptual thesis, he is in no doubt himself that a belief in the existence of objective values does figure in the everyday use of ethical terms. 'The ordinary user of moral language', he says,

---

[20] J. L. Mackie, *Ethics*, p. 18.

'means to say something about whatever it is that he characterizes morally, for example a possible action, as it is in itself, or would be if it were realized, and not about, or even simply expressive of his or anyone else's attitude or relation to it. But the something he wants to say is not purely descriptive, certainly nor inert, but something that involves a call for action, or for the refraining from action, and one that is absolute, not contingent upon any desire or preference or policy or choice, his own or anyone else's.'[21] When someone is in a state of moral perplexity, wondering, say, whether he ought to engage in work connected with bacteriological warfare, 'the question is not, for example, whether he really wants to do this work, whether it will satisfy or dissatisfy him, whether he will in the long run have a pro-attitude towards it, even whether this is an action of the sort that he can happily and sincerely recommend in all relevantly similar cases. . . . He wants to know whether this course of action would be wrong in itself. Something like this is the everyday objectivist concept of which talk about non-natural qualities is a philosopher's reconstruction.'[22]

It appears from this passage that Mackie is concerned not only to describe what he is probably right in taking to be the ordinary man's understanding of ethical terms, but also to point out that emotive, prescriptive, and naturalistic theories fail to do justice to it. He tends to imply that this is an objection to them, and of course, it would be an objection if their aim were simply to give an account of ordinary usage. But while this is often represented as their aim, it is not really so. No moral philosopher would simply acquiesce in the conclusion that, in so far as they imply the existence of objective values, all moral judgements are false, and leave it at that. He would rather give an account of moral judgements which supplied criteria, if not for their truth, at least for their acceptability; it would be a genuine but secondary consideration how far this account could be made to accord with ordinary usage. Mackie himself conforms to this procedure.

It would be simpler if one could analyse moral judgements realistically, accepting the existence of objective values, and leaving oneself only the task of marking and perhaps refining the distinctions among the uses of the words 'good', 'right', 'ought', 'must', and so forth. Why is this not possible? Mackie summarizes his case against

[21] Ibid., p. 32.   [22] Ibid., pp. 33–4.

the belief in the existence of objective values under five headings, but it boils down to two main arguments and a set of explanations for the prevalence of the false belief. The explanations, which I find convincing, consist in an invocation of the pathetic fallacy, our notorious tendency to project our feelings on to the objects which arouse them, combined with social and religious pressure to give what passes with us as moral conduct an objective sanction. The arguments are what Mackie calls the argument from relativity and the argument from queerness. The argument from relativity derives its force not just from the varieties of moral belief which are found in different ages, in different societies, and even among different persons with the same social backgrounds – for differences of opinion among natural scientists or historians are not taken as proof that there are no objective truths to be discovered in these domains – but rather from the fact that 'disagreement about moral codes seems to reflect people's adherence to and participation in different ways of life'.[23] The more powerful argument from queerness is that we are left in the dark as to what sort of things non-natural qualities can be, that we are equally uninformed about the relation which is supposed to hold between them and the natural qualities on which they are said to be supervenient, and that when we ask how their presence or absence is to be detected, we are told nothing more illuminating than that it is through a special faculty of moral intuition, being then left to wonder how the exercise of this faculty differs from the undergoing of a special feeling.

I find Mackie's reasoning persuasive. What puzzles me, however, is his conclusion that the belief in there being objective values is merely false, as if the world might have contained such things, but happens not to, just as it happens not to contain centaurs or unicorns. Whereas I think that the conclusion to which his argument should have led him is that the champions of objective values have failed to make their belief intelligible.

On this point, I side with Professor Hare, whom Mackie quotes as saying 'Think of one world into whose fabric values are objectively built; and think of another in which those values have been annihilated. And remember that in both worlds the people in them go on being concerned with the same things – there is no difference in the "subjective" concern which people have for things, only in

[23] Ibid., p. 36.

their "objective" value. Now I ask "What is the difference between the states of affairs in these two worlds?" Can any answer be given except "none whatever"?'[24]

Mackie objects that there would be a detectable difference, which would be reflected in moral argument. We have already remarked that the believer in objective goodness could not consistently embrace egoism, for he could give no reason why his portion of goodness should be given precedence over anyone else's, whereas for a subjectivist, egoism would be a coherent theory. There would be no inconsistency in advocating as a principle of conduct that each man should aim at the realization of his own interests. But this argument could be countered by our simply equating the belief in so-called objective goodness with the principle that, in default of special reasons, no one person's interests should count for more than anyone else's. It would then be left for us to decide whether this principle was acceptable. We should not decide this or any similar question arbitrarily, but rather in accordance with what we took to be the purpose of having a set of moral principles. The choice of these principles, out of which we may hope to succeed in framing a moral system, is then a responsibility that falls upon ourselves.

[24] Ibid., p. 21.

PART C: UTILITARIANISM

Since it is for us to decide what moral principles to adopt, it will be interesting to see whether there is any system with which we can be satisfied. One question which we shall have to tackle is whether anything of importance can be derived from the mere conception of morality. This is not to embark on an enquiry into what most people think they mean when they engage in what would ordinarily be classified as moral discourse. Whether or not they go so far as to believe that ethical terms stand for non-natural qualities, or that moral judgements derive their content and their authority from. divine commands, their theories about the status of morals are quite likely to be erroneous. This does not, however, absolve us from examining the data which such theories may be misrepresenting. We need to look at the circumstances in which moral judgements are made, the conditions under which they are found to be acceptable, which may vary considerably in different social climates, and the purposes which morality serves.

Three points which I am presuming to take for granted are that moral judgements are prescriptive in that they express or presuppose a favourable or unfavourable attitude towards certain forms of conduct, together with the dispositions from which these forms of conduct emanate, that the prescripts which they embody are applicable in different contexts, and that they are concerned primarily, though not exclusively, with the promotion of human welfare. I say 'not exclusively' because the welfare of other sentient beings and even the state of the natural environment may be treated as objects of moral concern.

None the less, I shall confine myself to human welfare, in order to simplify my discussion of utilitarianism, the moral theory which I am now proposing to examine. Though the theory has its sources in the work of earlier eighteenth-century writers like Helvetius, Hutcheson, and Hume, it owes its name to the Principle of Utility which was formulated by Jeremy Bentham in his *Principles of Morals and Legislation*, published in 1789. Its chief exponents in the nineteenth century were John Stuart Mill, who gave the title *Utilitarianism* to the book on ethics which he published in 1861, and the Cambridge philosopher, Henry Sidgwick, whose major work,

The Method of Ethics, came out in 1874. The theory was attacked by F. H. Bradley in his *Ethical Studies* and by G. E. Moore in his *Principia Ethica*, though Moore took the theory seriously enough to devote forty pages to expounding it in his later book, *Ethics*, which he contributed to the Home University Library in 1912. After being dormant for some time, the theory has recently come back into fashion.

One of the principal utilitarian tenets to which Moore also subscribes is that the rightness or wrongness of an action depends upon its consequences. In general, utilitarians are not interested in drawing fine distinctions between the use of different moral terms. In ordinary parlance, anything that ought to be done or that it is one's duty to do is right, but the converse does not hold. The class of right actions is treated as extending beyond the class of actions that one is under an obligation to perform, and this in its turn is treated as being wider than the class of one's duties. If I have promised to visit a friend in hospital, then I am thought to have put myself under an obligation to visit him. If I have not promised, I may be held not to be obliged to visit him, but it may be still thought right for me to do so as a kindly act. If I am his doctor, I may be said to have a duty to visit him which it would be wrong for me to neglect. These distinctions are not sharply drawn and one obligation or duty may conflict with another. Such cases of conflict are commonly resolved in an *ad hoc* fashion. One's duties are thought to depend in a large measure on one's station in life; one's obligations on one's own undertakings; but again, the division is not sharp. The nice shades of difference in the ordinary usage of words like 'must', 'ought', and 'should' supply material for the linguist but are of minor philosophical interest.

In any case, utilitarians disregard them. Their concern is in laying down rules of conduct and, as I have said, they look to consequences. The right action in any given situation is one that has or can be expected to have at least as good consequences as any other that is open to the agent, the consequences being taken to include any value that might attach to the action itself. I say 'has or can be expected to have' because it is not always made clear whether the rightness of an action is being made to depend on the totality of its actual consequences, or on the totality of its probable consequences, relatively to the information at the disposal of the agent, some or all of which may never become actual, or on those of its actual consequences that the agent may reasonably be expected to foresee. This is a question that we shall have to discuss later on.

Another doubtful point is whether its having the best consequences, or at least as good consequences as any feasible alternative, is to be regarded as a characteristic which happens to be common to all right actions or as one by which they are defined. The latter view is taken by Moore and on the face of it by Bentham, though we shall see that Bentham does not consistently adhere to it.

The second principal tenet of the eighteenth- and nineteenth-century utilitarians is, notoriously, that pleasure alone is intrinsically good and pain alone intrinsically evil. It follows that the right action is the one that causes or is calculated to cause at least as favourable a ratio of pleasure to pain as any other action that it would, in the circumstances, be open to the agent to undertake. Since these philosophers also identified degrees of happiness with the preponderance of pleasure over pain, their criterion of rightness was often represented as the tendency of an action to cause a greater degree of happiness than any alternative. It is because of this that Bentham, towards the end of his life, proposed to substitute the expression 'The greatest happiness principle' or 'The greatest felicity principle' for 'The principle of utility'.

cf:
Schopen-
hour

Unlike Moore, who went to considerable trouble to oppose the identification of good with pleasure, and also unlike Sidgwick, who treated the proposition that pleasure alone is good in itself as a synthetic truth, which was revealed to him by intuition, Bentham wrote as if he took the proposition to be analytic. At least this would seem to follow from his saying that unless pleasure is taken to be, in itself, a good, and pain, in itself, an evil, the words *good* and *evil* have no meaning. It is consistent also with his refusal to establish any hierarchy of pleasures. His measure of their value was purely quantitative, being determined by such factors as the intensity of a pleasure, its duration, and the width of its distribution. His inclusion of this last factor and his speaking, as he sometimes does, of the greatest happiness of the greatest number, must not mislead us into thinking that he admitted equality as an independent criterion of value. His point was only that in quantifying pleasures and pains, there was to be no weighting of persons; the feelings of everyone who was affected were alike to be taken into account.

A feature of his position which Bentham fails to make sufficiently clear is that it is not designed to supply individuals with moral guidance. There would, in his opinion, be no point in any such attempt, since guidance is useful only if it can be followed, and the individual was not credited by him with the power of choosing to do anything other than what he believed in the circumstances would secure the most pleasure for himself. Whatever may be the case with John Stuart Mill, Bentham did not rely upon the fallacious argument that since each man desires his own happiness, the general happiness must be desired by all. It is not impossible that someone should desire the general happiness, but he would need to be a person of a very altruistic nature, for whom the pursuit of the general happiness coincided with his own. Obviously there are very few persons of whom this is likely to be true.

Bentham's subtlety consists in his casting himself as one of them. He assumes the role of a legislator who has both the wish and the power to maximize the welfare of the society for which he legislates. He is, therefore, committed to the principle of utility. His task is to devise a political and legal system, besides creating a social climate, which will be most favourable for its exemplification in detail. It is to the fulfilment of this task, especially in its legal aspect, that Bentham's voluminous writings are devoted.

Not all legislators are benevolent and not all have the ability, even if they had the desire, to construct a beneficent system. The result has been the promotion of 'principles adverse to utility'. The two that Bentham mentions are the principle of asceticism and the principle of sympathy and antipathy, which he also denominates the principle of caprice. The principle of asceticism runs directly counter to the principle of utility, approving of actions in so far as they tend to diminish happiness and disapproving of them in so far as they tend to augment it. This principle is said by Bentham to have been embraced by two classes of persons whom he calls respectively moralists and religionists. In both cases, their motives have been egoistic. The moralists have sought to show themselves superior to the common run of men and so gain honours and admiration; the religionists by espousing the cause of pain in this world have hoped to avoid divine punishment in the world to come.

The principle of asceticism was said by Bentham to have been adopted by the Spartans as a measure of security. Otherwise, he did not think that it had played much part in matters of government. It was otherwise with the principle of sympathy and antipathy. This principle has chiefly served as a source of moral and political judgements. It ties such judgements to moral sentiments or intuitions, to feelings of approval or disapproval, or the deliverances of an alleged moral sense. Its use is considered by Bentham to be especially frequent and especially mischievous in the domain of the law, perhaps most of all in the infliction of punishment, for Bentham always a necessary evil, and in the distribution of rights. He does not suggest that those who apply the principle ever do so to the detriment of what they believe to be the greatest preponderance of pleasure that is obtainable for themselves.

But while Bentham's allowing for these deviant principles can most probably be reconciled with his psychological egoism, it does appear to run counter to his claim that it is only when they are interpreted in accordance with the principle of utility that words like 'right' and 'good' have any meaning. The reason for which he rejects the principle of sympathy and antipathy is that its operations are arbitrary. The moral and legal judgements which it yields are not subordinated to any objective criteria. This leaves them without any rational basis, but it does not render them meaningless. As for the principle of asceticism, since it is supposed to be the exact opposite of the principle of utility, it is represented by Bentham as giving an incorrect interpretation of the terms on which it is brought to bear, but not as depriving them of any meaning whatsoever. The actions which result from the application of the principle can be significantly, if wrong-headedly, described in moral and legal terms. What Bentham objects to is their disutility. It is for its having this effect and not for its misuse of language, that the principle is condemned.

By now it should be clear that when Bentham says it is only when they are used in a sense conformable with the principle of utility that words like 'ought', 'right', and 'wrong' have any meaning, he is not assuming the role of a lexicographer or even of a linguistic analyst. I doubt if he is even straightforwardly proposing that we make any radical change in our understanding of these words. He is crediting them with their usual normative force and trying to annex it to such states of affairs as are conformable to the principle of utility. When he says that it is only in that way that they acquire any meaning, what he is claiming is that there is no other descriptive meaning to which their normative force can be rationally attached.

In short, the principle of utility, in Bentham's hands, is a principle of the first order. It is not the outcome of an analysis of the use of moral, political, and legal terms. It is intended to be the guiding principle of a system of jurisprudence, with which both legal practice and moral judgements, with their respective sanctions, are to be brought into accord. It was not supposed by Bentham to be an entire innovation. The principle had been followed but only sporadically and not on any settled plan. Bentham envisaged it as a comprehensive instrument of reform.

If we are to meet Bentham on his own terms, the questions we must therefore ask are whether his system is practicable and whether it is desirable. Neither question is easy to answer. In the case of the first, the most common objections are that the principle of utility is sustained by a false psychology, and that even if it were not, its scientific pretensions would still be hollow. There could not be a felicific calculus. There is no way of summing the several quantities of pleasure and pain which are bestowed on a number of different people and putting the results in any sort of mathematical order.

Both these objections are well founded, but they do much less damage to Bentham's position than has commonly been supposed. Even if we confine ourselves to intentional actions, it is indeed false that they are always such as the agent thinks will bring him the greatest preponderance of pleasure. Much more often, he has some specific aim; to keep an appointment, to allay his curiosity, to solve a puzzle, to satisfy some physical need, to make mischief, to amuse the company, to gratify a friend. Such a list could be almost indefinitely extended. It may be objected that one would not engage in such activities unless it pleased one to do so, but the well-known rejoinder to this is that one needs to distinguish between the thought of an end to be pursued and the intentional object of the thought. From the fact that the thought is pleasurably flavoured, it does not follow that it has pleasure for its intentional object. It is not impossible that an object should be consciously pursued, not for its own sake, but for the sake of the pleasure which one expects to derive from obtaining it, but this is a sophisticated practice and if not altogether uncommon, by no means invariably the rule.

That ends other than happiness can be sought for their own sake is admitted in his *Utilitarianism* by Bentham's disciple, John Stuart Mill, though he has a tendency to suggest, as in the case of virtue, that such things start by being sought as means to happiness, and only subsequently become identified with it, or rather with one of its constituent parts. It should, however, not be overlooked, as it too frequently has been, that Mill admits the possibility of genuine self-sacrifice. After saying that the possibility of doing without happiness is proved by the fact that it is done involuntarily by nineteen-twentieths of mankind, he adds that 'it often has to be done voluntarily by the hero or martyr, for the sake of something which he prizes more than his individual happiness'.[25] This something is or should be 'the happiness of others or some of the requisites of happiness'.[26] I say 'or should be' because while Mill may regard this as the only justification for voluntary martyrdom he does not regard it as the only possible motive. 'All honour', he says, 'to those who abnegate for themselves the personal enjoyment of life, when by such renunciation, they contribute worthily to increase the amount of happiness in the world; but he who does it, or professes to do it, for any other purpose, is no more deserving of admiration than the ascetic mounted on his pillar. He may be an inspiring proof of what men *can* do but assuredly not an example of what they *should*.'[27]

There is no suggestion here that the ascetic is moved by the belief that the balance of pleasure will be redressed in his favour in a future life.

It has to be admitted that Mill is not consistent. Later on, in the same book, he claims to have shown 'that there is in reality nothing desired except happiness' and, having remarked that ultimate ends do not admit of proof, he was rash enough to argue that 'No reason can be given why the general happiness is desirable, except that each person, so far as he believes it to be attainable, desires his own happiness.'[28] There are passages where it seems not to matter to him whether he speaks of happiness or pleasure. Perhaps he was confused, perhaps only careless, but I am sure that the clue to what he principally thought is to be found in his distinguishing the quality of pleasure. His much quoted dictum that 'it is better to be a human being dissatisfied than a pig satisfied; better to be Socrates dissatisfied than a fool satisfied'[29] was not intended to imply that the pig or the fool enjoyed less pleasure. The criterion he was employing was that of enlightened preference. The fool or the pig might be of a different opinion, but 'it is because they only know their own side of the question'. Anyone who was in a position to see both sides would choose the other way in either case, even at the cost of pleasure. The example is not entirely felicitous, since it is not clear how a human

---

[25] J. S. Mill, *Utilitarianism*, Fontana Library Edition, p. 267.
[26] Ibid., p. 267.   [27] Ibid., p. 267.   [28] Ibid., p. 288.
[29] Ibid., p. 260.

being could know what it was like to be a pig, or vice versa, or how anyone could live both as a Socrates and as a fool, but we should not overcharge Mill for his rhetoric. What it comes down to is that everyone who has the capacity for enjoying 'the pleasures of the intellect, of the feelings and imagination, and of the moral sentiments' attaches a higher value to them than 'to those of mere sensation'.[30]

I do not know that this is true. I dare say that a counterexample could be found, but that does not matter for our present purpose. It is anyhow clear that Mill is generalizing his own scheme of values and expressing the hope rather than the knowledge that it is universally shared. The point of interest to us is that he supplies us with a criterion which will do equally well for Bentham. We are to devise a moral, legal, and political system, the realization of which will ensure that as many as possible of those who are affected by it obtain as much as possible of what they would prefer.

Since this is a normative principle, it does not need to be backed by psychological laws; it is enough that it be psychologically possible for it to be fulfilled. In fact, I do not believe that people, even when they are acting intentionally and freely, always do what they prefer. They are prevented by inertia, or bad habits, or social pretensions, or even by moral considerations to which they render homage, though it goes against the grain. It is no good saying that people would not yield to such influences unless they preferred to, for this would be to say no more than that their actions were intentional. We can be content with the tautology that when they are acting freely, they can do what they prefer and with the empirical fact that they indulge in their preferences more commonly than not.

Is such a system practicable? I think that it is so long as we treat our amended principle of utility, in Bentham's way, as a guide-line for legislation. Obviously, there is no possibility of attaining the kind of scientific accuracy that Bentham may have envisaged. At the same time, it is not very rash to assume that people wish to be assured of a reasonable standard of material comfort, that they prefer security of employment to enforced idleness, that they value freedom of speech and equality before the law, that they do not welcome interference in their private lives. It may be said that these are liberal ideals, which may not be applicable to all societies. To

[30] Ibid., p. 268.

take some obvious examples, not all communities are equally bound by tradition, nor do they attach the same value to equality or cherish the same conception of freedom. I am inclined to think that what I am calling liberal values would generally prevail, if they were given a fair run, but it is a question we can afford to leave open at this stage in the argument. All we need to claim is that those who are well acquainted with any given society, at least of the dimensions of a tribe, are able to sketch in broad outline the form of life which its members prefer, and can estimate the success of different measures in bringing it into existence and maintaining it.

I am afraid that we cannot have the same confidence when we pass from questions of government to those of individual morality. As I have already remarked, Bentham was not concerned with individual morality, except for the influence on conduct of social, legal, and political pressures, since he thought that men were bound to the pursuit of their own happiness; but John Stuart Mill, who differed from Bentham more radically than he admitted, looked to utilitarianism to serve as a moral touchstone and the same is true of all the subsequent utilitarians whose work is known to me.

When it comes to assessing personal conduct, we are supposed to draw a distinction between assessing the actual or probable consequences of some particular action and assessing the action or probable consequences of the general observance of some principle under which the action falls. I say 'actual or probable' because it makes a difference whether one is deciding what one ought to do in a given situation or passing judgement on some action which has already been performed. In the former case, unless one is simply going by rules, one is forced to rely on probabilities, or rather on what is known as mathematical expectation. The various merits of possible outcomes of different courses of action have to be blended with the various likelihoods of their occurrence and a decision based on the result. The fact that this could be a laborious procedure, and that one may well be left in doubt whether one has done the sum correctly, is an argument in favour of going by rule, especially when there is no conflict of well-entrenched principles.

When one is judging an action which has already been performed, one may try to follow Moore and others in making its rightness or wrongness depend upon its actual consequences. But this is not nearly so easy as one might think. Not only may many of its consequences still lie in the future, but it may be far from clear what its actual consequences have been, still less, what values ought to be attached to them. To revive an example, which I used many years ago in writing about Bentham's work,[31] was it right for Brutus and his fellow conspirators to kill Caesar? Can this be said to have led to the existence of the Roman Empire? If so, what verdict do we pass on the empire's achievements? How has its rise, decline, and fall, affected subsequent events? Are we to reckon the composition of Shakespeare's play, *Julius Caesar*, among the effects of Brutus's action? If we do, we have to measure the enjoyment it has given to thousands of readers and spectators against the sufferings of adolescents who have been forced to study it as a prescribed text. Clearly, we can raise a whole host of questions to which we should be at a loss for an answer. Not only that, but we are expected also to put a value on the alternatives to Brutus's acting as and when he did. What would have happened if Caesar had been allowed to die a natural death, and would the course of human history have been the better or the worse for it? What can one say to such questions except that they defy any rational answer?

The moral, as I see it, is that if we are judging actions after the event, and affecting to measure the rightness or wrongness of their actual consequences, we should treat such a verdict as a type of challenge. There will usually be a set of events, most often in the temporal neighbourhood of the action, which are readily allowed to pass for its effects. Someone claims that they constitute a more, or it may be less, satisfactory state of affairs than would have obtained if the action had been forborne. It is then for anyone who dissents to show that the consequences have been wrongly assessed or to argue the case for some more satisfactory alternative. What we can conclude is that, if the discussion is to be conducted along these lines, there is no sense in characterizing an action as right or wrong without further ado. We have to adduce the consequences on which we are basing the verdict and allow for the possibility of its being overridden.

In any case, if we are interested in personal morality, we are likely to be more concerned with finding some method of deciding what we ought to do than a yardstick for passing judgement on what is already done. It is established that only such consequences are relevant as the agent can reasonably be expected to foresee, but we

---

[31] See my *Philosophical Essays*, 'The Principle of Utility', p. 267.

have left it open whether we are to go by the probable consequences of each particular action or the usual consequences of the operation of some principle under which the action falls. The distinction in question is commonly known as that between act- and rule-utilitarianism. The practice of rule-utilitarianism seems much the easier and also has the apparent advantage of offering a way of escape from awkward examples. Thus, it might be suggested that it could be right to commit perjury to secure the conviction of an innocent man in a case where the man was a notorious source of mischief and there was no serious chance that one's perjury would come to light. But such a suggestion would be widely contested. There are many to whom such a course of action would be morally repugnant. We evade the difficulty by invoking the general rule. There is plenty of evidence that the resort to perjury to procure the conviction of innocent persons is in general a source of greater misery than satisfaction. Consequently, it should not be practised even in such conditions as those of our example.

Unfortunately, this way of escape is not readily accessible. The trouble is that the judgement which we hope to avoid by shifting from act- to rule-utilitarianism can always itself be represented as an instance of a rule. Suppose that one lives in a community where the custom of the vendetta is still in vogue and that one's sister has been seduced. Then on the basis of act-utilitarianism one may well conceive it to be one's duty to kill the seducer. The preferences of one's own kith and kin will be that the insult to their honour be avenged: this manner of avenging it may be thought satisfactory by the community at large: even the members of the seducer's family may agree that he deserved his fate, whether or not they feel bound to avenge him in his turn. Suppose now that someone takes a different moral view of this transaction and tries to sustain his case by aligning himself with the rule-utilitarians. What rule is he to invoke? That killing is wrong? This would hardly be admitted without qualification, though it is possible that total pacifism would be justified on utilitarian grounds. I know no way in which the question could be decided. That killing persons for no better reason than that they have seduced your sister, if adopted as a general practice, would run counter to more preferences than it satisfied? This might well be true, though it would be difficult to verify. But why should we come to rest at this point? If we made the rule a little more specific by adding the clause that the practice was to be adopted only in circumstances where the institution of the vendetta was held in esteem, the preference-count might very well be reversed. The resorting to rule would then deliver the same moral verdict as was reached by considering the most likely consequences of the particular act. There might be some point in stressing the distinction if one could make out a case for some optimum level of generality, but this does not seem feasible. The more specific the rule, the more likely it is to support one's intuitive assessment of the particular case in question. The more general it is, the less one has to enter into the actual circumstances and the easier it is, therefore, to apply.

In view of the collapse of the distinction between act-utilitarianism and rule-utilitarianism, we need to look a little closer at the thesis that moral judgements are capable of being universalized. This thesis is often said to be part of the logic of our use of moral terms and very large claims are made for it. That staunch prescriptivist, Professor R. M. Hare, who has also taken up the cause of utilitarianism, allows it to play a dominant part in what he calls his critical thinking. For instance, with the help of some unspecified facts, he uses it to obtain such debatable conclusions as that it is wrong to engage in extra-marital sex or that pacifist principles should not now prevail in the United States, still less in Israel. One would like to be shown the successive steps in the arguments which are supposed to establish these conclusions.

My own view is that next to nothing, beyond the conveyance of some emotive and prescriptive force, is to be extracted from the meaning of moral terms, once they are dissociated from pre-established standards. In particular, I think that the purely logical import of the universalizability attributed to moral judgements is nugatory. At the very least, it may be said, you must admit that an action which is right, or wrong, for a given person, in a given situation, must also be right, or wrong, as the case may be, for any other person in the same situation. But the problem is what is to count as the same situation. Any two situations are different in some respects, and if one is going to say that an action of a sort which it is right for A to perform in situation S, is also right for B to perform in situation S-, one has to assume that the differences between S and S-, not to speak of the differences between A and B, are morally irrelevant. This already takes us beyond the boundaries of logic.

One might think that the substitution of one token name for

another of nearly the same type, when the persons named are playing the same role, could make no moral difference, but even this would not be universally true. For instance, it does not appear wrong for a publisher to advertise a book by stressing the surname of its author. Yet, when, some years ago, the original publishers of *Language, Truth and Logic*, not being ignorant of the fact that its author, A. J. Ayer, is fairly well known as Freddie Ayer, brought out a rather poor detective story by an American, Frederick Ayer, and advertised it in England simply but obtrusively as Ayer's novel, I felt that they were morally culpable. If the American writer thought poorly of my philosophy, or perhaps philosophy in general, he might have felt a similar grievance. The point is that the publisher's action was not morally neutral.

In a recent book, *Moral Thinking*, Hare takes it as 'a conceptual truth that if I know that I would be prescribing something were I in exactly someone else's position with his preferences, I must now be prescribing the same thing with the same intensity'.[32] So far from accepting this proposition as a conceptual truth, I find it manifestly false. Were I in Mr Enoch Powell's position with his preferences, I should no doubt be recommending the return of coloured immigrants to their countries of origin, but to suppose that this commits me to propagating the same view with the same intensity is palpably ridiculous. According to Hare, 'To become moral is, first of all, to contemplate the hypothetical situation in which what are actually going to be states of another person would be states of one's self, and thus to acquire a hypothetical concern for the satisfaction of the preferences of one's self in that hypothetical situation; and then, because of universalizability, to find oneself constrained (unless one takes the amoralist escape route) to turn this merely hypothetical concern into an actual concern for the satisfaction of the preferences of the actual other person.'[33] The amoralist is not very clearly delineated, but he appears to be a person who refrains from making any universal prescriptions at all. It would be strange if there were nothing between that and taking on the persona of everyone with whom one has to deal. Perhaps amid the turmoil of preferences that one would then acquire, there is one that would prevail, but there is no guarantee that this would be so, and indeed no reason to believe that the whole exercise is feasible.

[32] Op. cit., p. 220.   [33] Ibid., p. 222.

The course of Hare's reasoning is difficult to follow, but his fundamental error seems to be the assumption that one can know what it is like for another person to entertain whatever preferences he does only to the extent that one can merge one's identity with his. It is indeed trivially true that if I were he, in the sense of being identical with him, I should have the preferences that he has; but this is a proposition from which nothing of interest follows. It certainly does not supply a basis for morality.

This is not to deny that utilitarianism can be moulded into a coherent policy, but only to rebut the claim that it is somehow imposed on us by the logic of moral discourse. It encounters the difficulty that it is not always easy to discover what the preferences of other persons are, but this is a difficulty which it shares with any moral theory which takes account of the effect of one's actions upon the feelings of others and I do not think that any moral theory which failed to do this would carry much conviction. There would, indeed, be nothing inconsistent about a policy of pursuing one's interest on all occasions: for what that is worth, it could be universalized; there is no contradiction in prescribing that everyone should be a thorough-going egoist. Even this would not dispense one from assessing the feelings of others, since they would have a bearing on one's own interests, but it would be much less than is required of the utilitarian who has to select a winner from the set of preferences which he can reasonably attribute to all those whom he can foresee that his action will affect. The objection to egoism is not logical but moral. It gives an undue advantage to the strong.

Are there no moral objections to utilitarianism, if we give its feasibility the benefit of the doubt? I think that there are. I do not see how a utilitarian could consistently avoid countenancing the oppression of minorities, the suppression of unpopular opinions, the sacrificing of justice to expediency. It is all very well to say that one would not opt for any of these things if one put oneself in the position of the victims, but this succeeds as a defence only if one overlooks the fact that one is also required to put oneself in the position of the victimizers who may well be more numerous than their victims and may greatly profit from their sufferings. Hare sometimes writes as if one should refrain from any action which is such that one would dislike being in the position of anyone whom it affected, but this would be carrying quietism to preposterous lengths. One could not even try to win a game which one knew that one's opponent would not be happy to lose. More seriously, it is not only the intensity of preferences that comes into question. Not all preferences are equally commendable.

I am prepared to go further. One reason why I have not developed the doubt whether the morality of universal concern is practicable is that I do not anyhow want to advocate it. I am in favour of what C. D. Broad called self-referential altruism. What this amounts to is very well put by Mackie in his *Ethics*. 'Concern for others, but for others who have some special connection with oneself; children, parents, friends, workmates, neighbours in the literal, not the metaphorically extended sense. Wider affections than these usually center upon devotion to some special cause – religious, political, revolutionary, nationalist – not upon the welfare of human beings in general.'[34] Mackie goes on to say that 'it is much easier, and commoner, to display a self-sacrificing love for some of one's fellow men if one can combine this with hostility to others', but I should hope that this could be avoided as a general rule. Not that I am preaching universal tolerance. There are always likely to be persons to whom one ought to be hostile: especially politicians, their masters, and their acolytes. I agree with Lord Acton that all power tends to corrupt and that absolute power corrupts absolutely.

A point which utilitarians tend to forget is that preferences do not come ready-made. They are the product of tradition, education, indoctrination, propaganda, prejudice, besides more-or-less enlightened self-interest and self-referential altruism. On this ground alone, they should not all be given equal weight. If a plebiscite were to be taken, I dare say that the majority of my countrymen would vote for the restoration of capital and corporal punishment, but this would not bring me over to their side, even if it could be shown that the fulfilment of their wishes would bring them a greater quantity of pleasure than the quantity of pain that it would cause.

But how do I justify my attitude? In this instance, by exposing the sadism which hides behind the profession of a concern for law and order, and by demolishing the theory of retributive punishment. In other instances, by using what appear to me to be the appropriate arguments. I have no all-purpose tool of justification. I suspect that my values do not significantly differ from the liberal values of John Stuart Mill, which means that they contain a strong utilitarian

---

[34] Op. cit., p. 132.

element but they do not fit neatly, any more than his did, into a utilitarian mould. Rather than pretend to the use of a system to which I cannot consistently adhere, I prefer to admit to being governed, as I believe that others are, by sympathy and antipathy; what Bentham unkindly called the principle of caprice.

2 On Causal Priority

In a chapter called 'The Direction of Causation' of his book *The Cement of the Universe*, John Mackie set out to answer two main questions. What is our concept of causal priority, of the direction of causation? and What, if anything, constitutes causal priority in the objects? In what real respect, if any, is the causal relation asymmetrical? He begins by remarking, quite correctly, that if one equates causes with necessary and sufficient conditions, there is no asymmetry. If *A* is both necessary and sufficient for *B*, then *B* is both sufficient and necessary for *A*. It is true that the relation between what he calls an Inus condition (an insufficient but non-redundant part of an unnecessary but sufficient condition) and its effect is not symmetrical, but it is not asymmetrical either. More often than not, if *A* is an Inus condition of *B*, *B* is also an Inus condition of *A*. Accordingly, regularity theories have drawn the conclusion that if there is to be any asymmetry, it can only be temporal. We simply make it a rule that causes must temporally precede their effects.

Mackie argues that this is at variance with our ordinary concept of causation. He gives three reasons.

1. We allow causes to be simultaneous with their effects as in Kant's example of a leaden ball making a hollow in a cushion, or the dependence in Newtonian physics of the acceleration of one body upon the masses and distances of other bodies at the same time. Not only that, but the idea of a cause succeeding its effects is not self-contradictory.

2. The relations of causal and temporal priority have different logical structures. Once a time direction has been given to any pair of events, it has been given to the system as a whole. In the series *A* to *E*, *C* comes betweeen *B* and *D*, whichever way the arrow goes. On the other hand, causal direction belongs, if at all, to each ordered pair on its own. *B* may be causally prior to *C*, while *D* and *E* might be causally irrelevant to each other, or *E* might be causally prior to *D*.

I confess that I do not see the force of this argument. Surely no one wants to maintain that A's being earlier than B is sufficient for A to be a cause of B, but only at most that it is necessary. The question whether causal and temporal priority are the same relation is badly framed. What is at issue is whether there is anything more to being a cause than being at least an Inus condition and having temporal priority, and to this the fact that A may be temporally prior to B without being an Inus condition of B is plainly irrelevant. The suggestion that the causal order may differ from the temporal order merely repeats the previous argument.

3. 'We regard causes as explaining their effects in a way in which effects do not explain their causes, and the mere fact of temporal priority would not account for this.'[1] Mackie reinforces this argument by remarking that, while the concurrence of two events or properties may be explained in certain cases by their being joint effects of the same cause, it is not thought to be explained by their being joint causes of the same effect; and the same applies to the case where the effect is overdetermined, in the sense that each of the causes was sufficient to produce it without the assistance of the others.

All this is true. It enters into our concept of cause and effect that the cause explains the effect, not vice versa. I take Mackie's point to be that if the relation between causes and effects were in all the other relevant respects symmetrical, then .the mere fact that causes preceded their effects would not lead us to draw this further distinction between them. It certainly would not if we were rational.

Let us assume, for the time being, that we are rational. On what ground, then, do we draw the distinction? Russell once suggested that the only asymmetry that could be considered relevant was an asymmetry in the correlations themselves. We take A's to be causally prior to E's when the relation is many–one, in the sense that there are other kinds of events B, C, D which are like A in being sufficient for E, whereas E is sufficient for either A or B or C or D. In that case, when instances of A and E occur in the absence of instances B, C, and D, the instance of A will be both sufficient and in the circumstances necessary for that of E, whereas the instance of E will be necessary for that of A but not sufficient, in the strong sense in which A is sufficient for E, since it might have been associated with an instance of B or C or D instead.

[1] *The Cement of the Universe*, p. 164.

This is a valid distinction, but Mackie objects that it is not the one that we ordinarily make in our assignment of causal priorities. Not only does it not account for our distinguishing between cause and effect when the relations are many–many and one–one, but even in cases where it pertains, it does not yield what we should regard as the right answer. Mackie gives as a counterexample the case of a slot-machine in which the insertion of a coin is correlated with several possible outcomes. If the causal direction were that of the many–one relation, we should say that the emergence of the bar of chocolate caused the coin to have been put in, but we are not in the least inclined to say this.

Mackie next considers a suggestion of von Wright's, that cause and effect are to be distinguished by means of the notion of action. In von Wright's words 'p is a cause relative to q, and q an effect relative to p, if and only if by doing p we could bring about q or by suppressing p we could remove q or prevent it from happening'.[2] To the obvious objection that many things other than human actions are believed to be causes, von Wright replies that very often these are things that we could have brought about or prevented, if we had been rightly situated, and that even when they are not we speak of them as though they were. This seems to me to be making rather too light of the difficulty.

Von Wright gets himself into further, and I think unnecessary, trouble by taking voluntary actions which are done directly, in the sense that they are not done by doing something else, to be causes without being effects. The neural processes on which such an action as raising my arm would ordinarily thought to be causally dependent are said by him to be the *effects* of my raising my arm, even though they are temporally prior. Only in the cases where the neural processes are actually brought about by the intervention of some physiologist does he allow the causal direction to go the other way. Mackie argues, and I agree with him, that given that von Wright has to appeal to possible actions anyway, he would have done much better to make the neural processes causally prior in all cases, on the ground that a physiologist could have organized or prevented them, whether or not one actually did so.

It is surprising that von Wright is so ready to admit temporally backward causation, since, so far as I can see, the only point in taking human action as the model is to ensure that causal and

[2] Ibid., p. 171.

temporal priority go together. This is because it seems obvious that what one brings about, or prevents, is something that happens or, but for being prevented, would have happened at a later time. But then let us look into this more closely. What is it to bring about a state of affairs *s*? It is to do something *x*, which is at least an Inus condition of *s*. Similarly, to prevent *s* is to do something *y* which is at least an Inus condition of not-*s*. But now there seems to be no good reason, on the face of it, why *x* should be earlier than *s* or *y* than not-*s*. My speaking French fluently is a sufficient condition of my having learnt it at some earlier time. My not speaking Russian is an Inus condition of my never having learned it. Then by speaking French do I bring it about that I have learned it? By not being able to speak Russian, do I prevent myself from having learned it? One is inclined to answer, surely not. You cannot bring about what has already happened. You cannot prevent what has already failed to happen. And this is not because you lack the requisite powers but because it makes no sense to talk in such ways. It makes no sense, because we take words like 'bring about' and 'prevent' in such a way that they look temporally forward. But if there is nothing more than that to it, all we need to do is a little unpacking. To bring about something *s* is to do something *x* which is (a) at least an Inus condition of *s* and (b) a process which starts at some time earlier than the occurrence of *s*. And now I coin the verb 'to calvinize', the relation of which to the actual doctrines of Calvin is of no consequence. To calvinize *s* is to do something *x* which is (a) at least an Inus condition of *s* and (b) a process which starts at some time later than the occurrence of *s*. Then what is the difference in efficacity between bringing *s* about and calvinizing *s*? So far I can see, none whatsoever.

Mackie displays no interest in the enormous amount of admittedly unintentional calvinizing that goes on; for reasons which I shall come to later, he would not regard the mass of it as a form of causation. He does, however, develop an example which he thinks might pass muster, or at least deserve consideration, as a possible instance of backward causality. The example is that of precognition where an earlier drawing, for instance, repeatedly prefigures a later pattern which is the product of some randomizing device. It is not necessary that the precognizing be a human action. It might be accomplished by a machine which included a photographic film. Instead of appearing on a photographic plate, the earlier arrangement might be exhibited by a set of iron filings on a flat sheet of glass. If *B* is the pattern foreshadowed, and *A* its foreshadowing, then what is requisite is that *A* and *B* should be too much alike for their resemblance to be a mere coincidence and that *B* should have a random origin which is such as to exclude both the hypothesis that it is caused by *A* and the hypothesis that *A* and *B* have a common cause.

An objection which has been raised by Professor Flew and others to any example of this sort, however well constructed, is that for the foreshadowed event to be the cause of its earlier model, it is necessary that it should come into existence. But it is always possible that in the interval between the two circumstances someone or something should prevent the foreshadowed item from coming into existence. Consequently, even in the case where it does exist, it cannot be accorded causal priority.

Mackie appears to regard this argument as cogent but I am not impressed by it. The premiss on which it depends is that *A* cannot be a cause of *B* if there might be circumstances in which *B* existed but *A* did not. But this rules out far too much. It requires that *A* be both necessary and sufficient for *B* which, as Mackie himself points out, is a much stronger condition than we ordinarily require for attributions of causality. For example, my reading Mackie's book was the cause of my paying attention to Flew's argument: but this is not to deny that there might have been circumstances in which I should have paid attention to Flew's argument, even though I had not read Mackie's book.

But, it may be objected, this misses the point. My reading Mackie's book set up a causal chain of which my writing this part of my essay is the fruit. The effect having arrived, one cannot do away with the cause, though one can imagine the event's proceeding from a different cause or even from no cause at all. But in the precognitive case, where the alleged effect is already on the scene, the alleged cause may still be prevented, and this is why this is not a genuine case of cause and effect.

But what does it mean to say that we can, or cannot, do away with the cause? Let us follow Mackie in taking as our precognitive example a drawing which matches a subsequent picture. Let us say that the drawing comes into existence at time *t* and the picture at time *t* + *n* and let *t* + *m* be a time between *t* and *t* + *n*. Then what is supposed to rule out the hypothesis that the existence of the picture causes the existence of the drawing is the conditional, admittedly unfulfilled in our example, that if such and such action had been taken at $t + m$ then the picture would not have come into existence at time $t + n$. But the same argument can be used in a case where the dating of the cause precedes the dating of the conditional. If I were, counterfactually, to believe at time t that Mackie's book contained nothing to interest me then I should not have embarked on it at time $t - n$. If I took any notice of Flew's argument at time $t + m$ it would be for another reason.

It may be objected that the cases are not parallel. Since I have read the book, nothing that anybody now does can make it the case that I have not read it. In the previous example, something could still be done to make it the case that the picture is not painted. But this objection carries no weight. Certainly if I have read the book nothing that anyone does will make it true that I have not read it. But equally, if the picture will be painted, nothing that anyone does will make it true that it will not be painted. The most that one can say is that if such and such things were to be done or foreborne the picture would not be painted. But then we can equally say that if such and such things were now being done or foreborne I should not previously have read the book. Future events cannot be prevented for the logical reason that if they are prevented they will not occur and so are not future events, any more than past events which have been calvinized can fail to have been so. Future events could be prevented in the sense that if something which is not happening or going to happen were to happen they would not occur, but in exactly the same way past events could avoid being calvinized. There is no asymmetry here, only an obstinacy in insisting that causes should precede or at the very least not succeed their effects.

Mackie himself takes a rather more flexible view. He proposes to define causal priority in terms of fixity. C is to be regarded as causally prior to E if and only if C is at least an Inus condition of E and it is not the case that E is fixed at a time when C is not fixed. But what meaning is attached here to 'being fixed'? The answer is that one of two conditions must be satisfied. An event is to count as being fixed only when it has occurred or some sufficient condition of it has occurred. This allows a small margin for backward causation since there might be three events, or sets of events, A, B, and C, listed in temporal order, such that A, occurring at time t, was sufficient for C, that nothing occurring at or before time t, was sufficient for B, and that C was an Inus condition of B. C could not be more than an Inus condition of B, since if it were a sufficient condition then B would already be fixed at t, through the chain of sufficient conditions, A, C, B.

The simple identification of causal with temporal priority is thus avoided by allowing events to be fixed independently of the time of their occurrence by the occurrence of sufficient conditions for them. But now it looks as if the remedy is going to be worse than the disease, since whenever the cause is a sufficient condition, its effect becomes fixed at the same time as the cause, and how are we then to assign the causal priority? The difficulty is most baffling in the case where the alleged cause is both sufficient and necessary for the alleged effect. For then the sufficient relation between the events is symmetrical so that they are fixed simultaneously. Since we are not permitted to invoke mere temporal priority, it seems to become quite arbitrary which we count as the cause and which the effect.

Mackie is aware of this difficulty and tries to meet it by saying that while the causal priority of X to Y, in a case where X is sufficient for Y, is not revealed by any difference in the fixity of X and Y, the unfixity of the relevant circumstances may reveal it. 'Otherwise', he adds, 'we must fall back either on our experience of interventions, or on the continuity of causal processes.'[3] But if the relevant circumstances are unfixed, they have not occurred. And if it is not X alone but the conjunction of X and C that is sufficient for Y, then if C has not occurred Y is not fixed, unless by some other sufficient condition. But the difficulty which Mackie is trying to meet is posed by the case in which Y *is* fixed through the fixing of X, so that the relevant circumstances cannot be unfixed. As for our falling back on our experience of intervention, this is just to revert to von Wright's theory, which we have already found to be unsatisfactory. Neither can I see what is gained by an appeal to the continuity of causal processes. It is not even clear to me what this amounts to. The only clue that we get from Mackie is that 'even if X is sufficient for Y, it may be plain that some continuous process of movement or change, starting from some other event Z that was unfixed until it occurred, led on to X and only through X to Y'.[4] But what is the force here of 'only through X'? If it means that X was necessary as well as sufficient for Y it does not affect the issue, since Y would then be sufficient as well as necessary for X. We are left with nothing to fall

[3] Ibid., p. 182.   [4] Ibid.

back on but temporal priority. I suppose that what Mackie had in mind was that there are some processes, like the progress of a disease, which it is natural for us to view as developing causally in a temporally forward direction. But this is to abandon the criterion of fixity in favour of the quite different criterion of the way in which we find it natural to arrange events; and that still remains to be explained.

One of the ways in which we find it natural to arrange events is embodied in a principle which Mackie adds to his criterion of fixity in giving his final account of our concept of causal priority. As he expresses it, the principle runs: 'If there is some central event A, and somehow causally connected with it some dispersed order item B – that is, some collection of separate events B_1, B_2, B_3, etc., whose co-occurrence is intrinsically improbable and calls for explanation – so that A is prior to B with respect to the dispersal of order, and there is no other central event that can be related to B_1, B_2, B_3, etc., so as to explain their co-occurrence, then this is evidence that A is causally prior to B; the reason being that A is apparently the only available explanation for the co-occurrence, but it can explain this only if it is the causally prior item.'[5] The last clause of this quotation appears superfluous, since the only claim A has to being the causally prior item, is that it appears to be the only available explanation for the Bs. I take exception, too, to talk of things being intrinsically improbable, unless no more is meant than that they show a marked deviation from the *a priori* distribution of chances. It is the neglect of this proviso that vitiates much of what is said about extra-sensory perception. Not but what we are more inclined to require an explanation when events do not conform to the *a priori* distribution of chances than when they do. I see this, however, as no more than a prejudice.

Mackie remarks, correctly, that it is not logically necessary that the dispersal of order should go forward in time. It could be and sometimes is the other way about. It just happens to be the case that it most often does go forward. This gives us some justification for assimilating causal to temporal priority, though not for making this a universal rule.

I should make it clear that in the passages which I have summarized, Mackie has been concerned only to explicate the

---

[5] Ibid., p. 190.

concept of causal priority which he thinks that we actually entertain, in the way that an anthropologist might examine the concept of witchcraft which was current in some native tribe. He does not commit himself to saying that the concept is actually satisfied. On the contrary, he thinks that if determinism is true, and if there was no first event, then our concept of causal priority has no application. The reason for this is that under those assumptions no event would ever be unfixed. Every event would be fixed by the existence of a preceding sufficient condition. On the other hand, if there were a first event, for instance an act of creation, by which every subsequent event was determined, then the concept of causal priority would have application. X would be causally prior to Y if it lay on some causal line between Y and the original initially unfixed event. Our actual attributions of causal priority would, however, frequently be false, since they would imply that events were unfixed when they were really fixed.

Much of this is puzzling. If, as Mackie believes, his concept of causal priority is contained in our ordinary concept of causation and this concept of causal priority does not apply to anything, then our concept of causation does not apply to anything either. I shall, in fact, be arguing that there is a good deal to be said for this conclusion, but it does surprise me that our ordinary concept of causation should be held to be inconsistent with determinism. For what is determinism if not the doctrine that every event has a cause? It would seem that Mackie equates it with the doctrine that every event has a sufficient condition, but it still comes as a shock that this should be taken to entail that no event has a cause. The mischief lies in the assumption that for any event to have a cause, some event must be unfixed. It is not evident to me, however, that this assumption is built into our ordinary concept of causation or even that Mackie's own account of causal priority requires it. It would require it if he made it a condition of X's causing Y not only that there can be no time at which X is unfixed and Y fixed but also that there must be a time when X is fixed and Y unfixed, but he explicitly declines to adopt this second condition. Why then does he develop his argument as though he had adopted it?

I think that the trouble consists in his saddling himself with von Wright's criterion as a means of ensuring that X will be causally prior to Y when X is both earlier than Y and a sufficient condition of Y. This leads him to found the concept of causation on the idea of human agency. If one then makes the assumption that the things which we bring about are not fixed until we bring them about, one is led to the conclusion that unless some things are unfixed, our concept of causation is vacuous.

But why should we make this assumption? It entails not just that the things which we bring about would not have happened in the existing circumstances unless we had acted as we did, but that our actions themselves were unfixed until they were done. For if they had been fixed beforehand, that is to say, if there had been sufficient conditions for them, the fixity of the conditions would have extended to the actions as their consequences. In short, the assumption is that we cannot properly be said to bring anything about unless we act freely, and act freely moreover in a sense that requires that our actions lack sufficient conditions. In treatments of the question of free will it has sometimes been argued that the attribution of freedom presupposes causality, in the sense that our choices are both causes and effects. Now we have the converse thesis that the attribution of causality presupposes free will.

I feel no call to decide how far this thesis runs contrary to common sense. It does seem plausible to surmise that the causal concepts which were developed by our remote ancestors originated in their experiences of action and not implausible to credit them with the belief that many of their actions were spontaneous. On the other hand, it also seems likely that with the spread of scientific information the concept or concepts of causality which are generally prevalent are not wholly anthropocentric. The belief in determinism was quite widely held in the nineteenth century, and it certainly was not thought to be incompatible with causality.

For this reason, I am inclined to doubt whether our concept of causal priority, and consequently our concept of causation, does require, as Mackie thinks it does, 'that there is a real contrast between the fixity of the past and the present and the unfixity of some future events, free choices or indeterministic physical occurrences, which become fixed only when they occur'.[6] In any case, I think that we have to distinguish two different contrasts here. There is the contrast between events for which there are sufficient conditions and indeterministic events, whether mental or physical, which may occur at any time, and the quite different contrast

---

[6] Ibid., p. 191.

between events which have occurred or are currently occurring and events which have not yet occurred. I believe, in opposition to Mackie, that the validity of the first of these contrasts is not required by our ordinary concept of causation, which leaves it an open question whether there are any undetermined events. On the other hand, I think that the second contrast is required, since I take it to be a common-sense belief that causal and temporal priority generally go together, or in other words, that the past determines the future in a way that the future does not determine the past. I am not going so far as to say that the idea of temporally backward causation passes for being self-contradictory, but I think that the cases in which it would be admitted, even as a possibility, are at least very rare.

While I doubt whether the common-sense concept of causality is still so largely anthropocentric as von Wright and Mackie make it out to be, I think that it remains anthropocentric to the extent of incorporating the idea that by and large the past brings about the present and the present brings about the future. There is thought to be a general direction of efficacity which coincides with the march of time. And if this is a fair account of it, then I want to go even further than Mackie to the point of asserting that the common-sense concept of causality is certainly not satisfied. My contention is that there is no efficacity in nature and consequently no direction of efficacity either. There are just more-or-less regular patterns of occurrences, which we choose to pick out, and these patterns can in most cases be read just as well backwards as forwards in time. There may be reasons of convenience for selecting many–one relations or for making the less orderly states of a system a function of the more orderly, and it may be that these asymmetries most often exhibit a forward direction in time, but that they do so is only a contingent matter, nor is it invariably the case.

But even if our addiction to explaining the later in terms of the earlier does not reflect any natural constraint it still needs to be accounted for. No doubt it is partly due to the prevalent illusion that our actions necessitate their consequences in some mysterious way that amounts to more than their being systematically correlated with them, but this illusion is not, I think, the only factor, besides calling for explanation in its turn. I suggest that a deeper reason is that we know, or believe ourselves to know, so much less about the future than we do about the present and the past. For our desire for explanation is bound up with, even if it is not exhausted by, our desire to extend our knowledge. We want to use our theories to arrive at true beliefs about particular events or facts of which we do not have previous knowledge, and in the vast majority of cases this amounts to our wanting to make true forecasts. Consequently, when we find it convenient to correlate an element of the less well-known domain with one of the better known we treat it as the junior partner. We conceive of what is later and so less likely to be revealed before it occurs as being dependent on what is earlier and so relatively more likely to have been ascertained, and we then generalize this tendency and project it upon nature.

This conclusion may be easier to accept when it is realized that we are anyhow imposing an order upon nature whenever we make a causal judgement. The regularities, on the basis of which such judgements are justified, do indeed obtain, at least so far as we can tell, but it is we who select them and attach significance to them. In Mackie's view, which I share, causal statements, to the extent that they do anything more than give accounts of actual regularities, are unfulfilled conditionals and to the extent that they are unfulfilled conditionals they are statements of fiction. The facts are that events of various kinds stand in such and such spatio-temporal relations to one another. Statements about what would or would not happen in non-existent circumstances are not statements of fact. They have to do with what C. S. Peirce called the arrangements of fact. They are pieces of fiction which illustrate the way in which we find it convenient to think that the world works. So if it suits us to tell stories in which earlier events exercise a hold over later events which is not reciprocated, we are not doing any violence to the facts; but we are not doing any special justice to them either.

3   The Causal Theory of Perception

My excuse for initiating a fresh discussion of what many regard as the stale topic of the causal theory of perception is that I do not believe that the various questions which it raises have been sufficiently disentangled or that satisfactory answers to all of them have yet been found.

The background to the theory, in all its forms, is the scientific account of the ways in which physical objects come to be perceived by us. To take a simple example, it is accepted that at least part of the causal explanation of my seeing what I identify as this piece of paper is that light proceeding from a physical object of the appropriate sort irradiates my eyes and that certain processes consequently take place in my brain. It may be disputed whether a set of sufficient conditions for the perception to occur would need also to include an irreducibly mental factor, but it is agreed that such physical conditions are necessary. The truth of the scientific account is nowadays not put in question. What comes up for discussion is its philosophical implications.

Let us begin then by considering what these implications have been thought to be. I distinguish eight different theses which have either been taken for the causal theory of perception or thought to be comprised in it. Some of them may be held in combination but not all of them are mutually compatible.

1. It has been asserted that what we must mean by saying that someone perceives a physical object of such and such a sort is that he is undergoing some sense-experience which the object in question causes. This is the thesis which Professor Price, for example, takes the causal theory to consist in when he discusses the theory in his book *Perception*. He expresses it in his own terms by making the causal theorist maintain that the relation of 'belonging to' which obtains between a 'sense-datum' and the physical object which the sense-datum 'presents' is the relation of 'being caused by'.[1] A

[1] H. H. Price, *Perception*, p. 66.

variant of this thesis which may be adopted by philosophers who would like to do away with sense-experience and *a fortiori* with sense-data consists in taking the effect to be the holding of some belief. Usually this belief will be, or at any rate comprise, the belief that the physical object in question exists, but this cannot always be so, since it must be allowed that for someone to perceive a physical object of such and such a sort is consistent with his misidentifying it.

2. It may be denied that any reference to causality enters into the meaning of the sentences which are used to state that someone perceives a physical object, but nevertheless held that the object's playing its causal role is a necessary condition for any such statement to be true. Here again different views may be taken of the character of the effect.

3. Almost invariably, those who hold either of these first two theses also hold that we frequently know, or at least have very good reason to believe, in particular cases that the relevant causal condition is satisfied. This is implied by their holding that we frequently know, or at least have very good reason to believe, that some particular statement of perception is true.

4. It would, however, be possible to hold either of the first two theses, while also holding that we had no good reason to believe that the causal condition was satisfied, or even holding that it never could be satisfied. If Hume can be thought to have held that those who adopted what he called the 'philosophical system' with regard to physical objects were so deluded as to make their perceptual statements accord with it, then something like this thesis can be attributed to him.

5. Conversely, it may be held that at least the majority of our perceptual statements are literally false, because they run counter to the causal condition. This was, for example, the position taken by Prichard. He thought that the ordinary meaning of sentences which are used to state that someone sees or touches a physical object was such as to commit us to naïve realism, and that the scientific account of perception, among other things, showed naïve realism to be false. What happens, as he put it, is that one sees a colour and 'straight off mistakes it for a body'.[2] This would not automatically disqualify the perceptual statements which are derived from the other senses, since they at least are commonly interpreted in causal terms. I think,

---

[2] *Vide* H. H. Price, 'Obituary of Harold Arthur Prichard', *Proceedings of the British Academy* XXXIII.

however, that Prichard might well have argued that they too were false, on the ground that the bodies to which we refer in ordinary speech as the sources of sounds or tastes or smells are not the physical objects that actually produce them but the non-existent bodies which we mistakenly suppose ourselves to see and touch.

6. Some philosophers, who are sufficiently indulgent to common sense to admit an interpretation of perceptual statements which will allow them to be true, have nevertheless been convinced by the scientific account of perception that physical objects are in themselves very different from what they appear to us to be. A moderate version of this thesis was put forward by Locke when he distinguished between primary and secondary qualities, supposing that our ideas of the primary qualities of solidity, extension, figure, number, rest, and motion resemble qualities which the objects literally possess, whereas our ideas of the secondary qualities of colour, sound, smell, and taste do not, the secondary qualities being, in his view, 'nothing in the objects themselves, but powers to produce various sensations in us by their primary qualities, i.e. by the bulk, figure, texture and motion of their insensible parts'.[3] From this it would seem to follow that physical objects may not play us very false in the way that they present themselves to our sense of touch, though, not being literally coloured, they cannot be very like the way they look.

In more recent times, the most prominent defender of this thesis has been Bertrand Russell, who carries it further than Locke. For instance, I think that Locke most likely belonged to the company of those whom Russell accused of clinging to naïve realism to the extent of locating physical objects in perceptual space. Russell himself referred to 'the construction of one space in which all our perceptual experiences are located' as 'a triumph of pre-scientific common sense' but still took common sense to be in error in supposing that it had discovered the whole truth about space. 'An even more serious error,' he continued, 'committed not only by common sense but by many philosophers, consists in supposing that the space in which perceptual experiences are located can be identified with the inferred space of physics, which is inhabited mainly by things which cannot be perceived.'[4] It is only, therefore, in a 'Pickwickian sense', according to Russell, that I 'see' the

[3] John Locke, *An Essay Concerning Human Understanding*, II, ch. viii, sect. 10.
[4] Bertrand Russell, *Human Knowledge: Its Scope and Limits*, p. 220.

furniture in my room. Unlike the visual and tactual table which is constructed out of percepts, the physical table is a wholly inferred entity. It is allowed to have some similarity in structure to the perceptual table, but though it is not at all clear what Russell took this similarity to be, I doubt if he let it go so far as Locke's matching of primary qualities with our ideas of them.

7. Russell is not the only philosopher to have drawn conclusions of this sort from the scientific account of perception, but I believe him to be unique in taking the further step of assigning to perceptual space and all its contents a physical location in the percipient's head. For all the apparent strangeness of this doctrine, he regarded it as an obvious consequence of what he termed the causal theory. 'Whoever,' he said, 'accepts the causal theory of perception is compelled to conclude that percepts are in our heads, for they come at the end of a causal chain of physical events leading, spatially, from the object to the brain of the percipient. We cannot suppose that, at the end of this process, the last effect suddenly jumps back to the starting-point, like a stretched rope when it snaps.'[5]

8. For the most part, those who have held that both our ordinary perceptual statements can properly be construed in a way that allows them to be true, and that the existence of the appropriate causal relation between the percipient and the physical object which he perceives is at least a necessary condition of their truth, have also taken our perception of physical objects to be indirect. That is to say, they have contrasted physical objects as inferred entities with the sense-data, or percepts, or whatever, which are supposed to be immediately presented to us. It is, however, to be remarked that this conclusion is not entailed by their premises. It is possible also to impose the causal condition upon a phenomenalistic or even a naïve realist account of perception. Indeed, I shall be arguing that it is only in this sort of way that the causal condition is acceptable at all.

In discussing these theses, I shall not devote any space to the variants of the first two of them in which an attempt is made to do away with sense-experience. I take it for granted that we do see colours and that a sentence such as 'This is red' does not mean anything even roughly like 'A normal percipient would not easily pick this out of a clump of geranium petals though he would pick it out of a clump of lettuce leaves.'[6] Any suggestion of this kind too

[5] Bertrand Russell, *The Analysis of Matter*, p. 320.
[6] Cf. J. J. C. Smart, 'Sensations and Brain-Processes', *Philosophical Review* LXVIII.

obviously puts the cart before the horse. This does not commit me to denying that an event which consists in someone's seeing a colour can be identical with an event in his brain. I do not in fact think that any sufficient reason has yet been given for believing that there are such identities, but I am content to leave the question open. It does not arise in the present context except for those who hold what I regard as the mistaken view that physical causes can have only physical effects.

In saying that I take it for granted that we do see colours, I am not denying the possibility of our seeing coloured objects, nor ruling out any suggestion as to what sorts of objects these might be. It is, indeed, clear that philosophers, like Russell, who adopt what one may call a 'two-world theory' are committed to the introduction of something of the order of sense-data, and nowadays this tends to be regarded as a fatal flaw in their position. My own view is that it is rather one of its merits. If I do not pursue this question here, it is because I have nothing new to add to the reasons which I have elsewhere given for holding that the insertion of what I now call sensory qualia into the analysis of perception is not only legitimate but advantageous.[7] I should resume them, if the question affected my argument, but my discussion of the two-world theory will follow a different course.

Can any of the eight theses be dismissed out of hand? The most obvious candidates are the fourth and fifth. Whether or not we believe that the causal condition enters into the meaning of our everyday perceptual statements, it seems absurd to say that we have no ground for accepting any of them, still more that they are all false. Surely this would be too much of an affront to common sense. But is it absolutely out of the question that the common-sense view of the nature of physical objects should be radically confused? And if it were shown to be so, what should be our assessment of the truth-value of the statements which embodied it?

This last question is one that I find difficult to answer. An imaginary example which I am fond of using is that of the members of a tribe whose belief that all natural occurrences are due to the moods of their deity is reflected in their language. So, in the circumstances in which we should say that it was raining, they say that Mumbo Jumbo is sad. Suppose we do not believe in the

[7] For example in *The Central Questions of Philosophy*, ch. IV.

existence of Mumbo Jumbo, or even believing in his existence, do not believe that the rain is an expression of his grief. Are we to conclude that what they say is false? It might seem that we must, if we are to hold by our own beliefs. On the other hand there is surely a sense in which the state of the weather does settle the question whether Mumbo Jumbo is sad or cheerful; if it does rain, those who have predicted that Mumbo Jumbo would be sad have, in this sense, been proved to be right. If one held a strictly verificationist theory of meaning, one might maintain that what the tribesmen really meant by saying that Mumbo Jumbo was sad was just that it was raining, and in that case one need not hesitate to allow that what they say is true. The trouble is that this hardly seems to do justice to their culture. Perhaps we should compromise by saying that what they assert can be true on their own terms, though those terms themselves are unacceptable.

Now, whatever Berkeley may have thought, the ordinary man in our culture is surely a naïve realist. He believes that he sees and touches physical objects, in a straightforward way which does not leave room for any intermediaries, and he also believes that the physical objects which he sees and touches continue to exist at times when nobody perceives them. Not only that, but I take it to be a common-sense belief that in very many cases these objects continue to exist in very much the same form as that in which they normally are perceived. This would imply, among other things, that they retain their colour in a literal sense which cannot simply be equated with their power to produce sensations of colour in us. Empirical research might show that the spread of scientific information had weakened this belief, but I should be surprised if it were not found still to be prevalent. At any rate I am going, for the sake of the argument, to assume that this is so. Suppose then that we were persuaded of the truth of the two-world theory or anyhow of the validity of something like Locke's distinction between primary and secondary qualities. We should have to conclude that there just were no such objects as the ordinary man believes that he sees and touches. It would not be true of anything both that it was straightforwardly perceptible through the senses of sight and touch and that it enjoyed 'a continued and distinct existence'[8] in the form in which it was perceived. So when people referred to such objects,

---

[8] Cf. David Hume, *A Treatise of Human Nature*, I, pt. iv, sect. 2.

as we are assuming that they constantly do, there would be a good reason for concluding that all that they said was false. On the other hand it would, so to speak, not all be equally false. There would still be a sense in which someone who claimed to have seen the Albert Memorial in London could be held to be right as opposed to someone who claimed to have seen it in New York.

In this case, and perhaps also in the other, though the greater waywardness in our eyes of the Mumbo Jumbo people would put a greater strain upon our tolerance, the plausible equation of meaning with truth-conditions favours a principle of charity. If the circumstances in which the members of some class of statements are commonly accepted are thought by us to be describable in such a way as to make the statements generally come out true, then we are disposed to treat such descriptions as yielding the meaning of these statements, whatever their authors may actually have had in mind. Even if our theory of meaning makes provision for the authors' intentions, the intentions which we attribute to them need not be any that they ever consciously have. They are supposed to want to make their audience believe what we in our greater wisdom would regard as verifying what they say.

As I said before, I am not sure how far this attitude is justified. If we are mainly concerned to discover what someone means by an assertion, we should presumably take some account of his own view of its truth-conditions. At the same time we want to allow for the possibility of his being mistaken about his meaning. For instance, if someone is convinced that when he talks about himself he is referring to a spiritual substance, we may well want to deny that there are, or could be, spiritual substances, without wanting to deny the truth of everything that he says about himself. In such a case we should most probably invoke the distinction between meaning and analysis, which permitted Moore to maintain his defence of common sense, while leaving it open for common-sense statements to receive interpretations which the ordinary man would never think of giving them. This may, indeed, be a distinction that we cannot afford to do without, but I do find it tenuous. It is not at all clear to me where meaning stops and analysis begins.

I am anyhow disposed to think that the question of meaning is here of secondary importance. What we have primarily to decide is whether the scientific account of perception obliges us to view the facts in any such way as philosophers like Locke and Russell have supposed. Do we have to conclude that physical objects are identifiable only as causes which are known to us only through their perceptible effects? Do we have to draw something like Locke's distinction between primary and secondary qualities? What distinction, if any, are we entitled to make between physical and perceptual space? When we have answered such questions as these, it will be time to consider how far the picture of the world that emerges is different from any view that we could reasonably attribute to common sense and how much charity we think it proper to expend for the purpose of bringing common sense into line. If my reasoning is correct, it will in fact turn out that very little charity is needed, even to accommodate a causal condition.

The first point for which I wish to argue is that it cannot be the case both that we have good reason to believe in the existence of physical objects and that the only means by which any of them can be identified is as the literally unobserved cause of some perceptible effect. I am not excluding the possibility that some physical objects can legitimately be identified in this way: I do not, for example, wish to deny that astronomers had good reason to believe in the existence of the planet Neptune before it was actually observed. I am not saying even that we can never be justified in referring to unobservable entities. I am not, in fact, convinced that the most minute of physical particles are unobservable in principle, but even if they were, I should not wish to deny that the part which they play in causal explanations would give us what is both a good reason and the only reason that we have for believing in their existence. What I am saying is that this cannot be true of physical objects in general.

This should become clear when we consider what the contrary view implies. It requires us to maintain, first, that the features of our actual sense-experiences, taken by themselves, make it probable that they have external causes, secondly, that these external causes, situated in a space of their own, bear at least a structural correspondence to what it seems to us that we perceive, and thirdly, that we are able to differentiate among these causes in a way that allows us to pick out one of them, or possibly one group of them, as a so-called object of perception and treat the others as conditions which also serve to make the perception possible. For the better development of my argument I shall take these propositions in reverse order.

That my third proposition at least presents a difficulty for the causal theorist is already well known. Professor Price once suggested that the difficulty could be met by drawing a distinction between what he called 'standing' and 'differential' conditions,[9] but Professor Grice, in his celebrated essay on 'The Causal Theory of Perception', has shown that this is insufficient. As he pointed out, a source of illumination may be a differential condition in a situation where we should not be willing to identify it as the object perceived. Grice's own suggestion was that 'the mode of causal connexion' should be indicated by examples. He advised his causal theorist 'to say that, for an object to be perceived by X, it is sufficient that it should be causally involved in the generation of some sense-impression by X in the kind of way in which, for example, when I look at my hand in a good light, my hand is causally responsible for its looking to me as if there were a hand before me, or in which . . .'.[10] But the trouble with this is that such an example only works if it is already established that I am looking at my hand, that is to say, in terms of the theory, if it is *already* established that there is just one external object, referred to as 'my hand', which is causally responsible for the relevant sense-impression in the distinctive way required. It cannot possibly be a method of *introducing* such an object. This may not be an argument against Grice, since it is not clear that he was concerned with a causal theory of the type that I am now discussing, but it does show that he offers no help to anyone who does hold such a theory.

Much the same argument holds against the suggestion, which has also been made, that the distinctive cause can be identified by specifying the part that it plays in the causal story. In Grice's example, my hand would be singled out as the one and only object that in such and such circumstances transmits light-waves to my eyes. The usual objection to this proposal is that it is not open to us to incorporate the details of a scientific theory into an analysis which is intended to capture the meaning of ordinary statements of perception, but whatever force this objection may have, it does not apply here since we have put aside the question of fidelity to common sense: we are concerned only with the inferences that we may or may not be entitled to make. What seems to me the decisive objection is again that the parade of scientific detail requires that the physical objects in question, the hand from which the light is

[9] *Perception*, p. 70.
[10] H. P. Grice, 'The Causal Theory of Perception', *Proceedings of the Aristotelian Society*, Supplementary Volume XXXV (1961), p. 143.

transmitted and the eyes which receive it, should already have been identified. It cannot serve to introduce them. They cannot simply be identified as *the* external causes of such and such perceptible effects, because the whole point of bringing in the scientific story is to inform us *which* these otherwise unknown causes are.

Not only must such objects already have been identified, but they must also have been located. The scientific story will not enable us to pick out the right objects unless we can fix the beginning and the end points of the path which the light is said to follow. And how can we possibly do this unless they are situated in a space of which the occupants are literally perceptible? How could we conceivably find them in a counterpart space, which is a purely inferential construction, a space which is not even generated out of perceptible items? To be applicable at all, the scientific story requires that my hand be *here*, where I see it, not somewhere in a postulated space which is closed to observation. There are, indeed, cases in which scientific theory leads us to correct our untutored estimates of distance; for instance, we conclude that the sun is very much further away from the earth than it appears to be: but the space to which these corrections refer is still a space of which the occupants are perceptible, and the scientific theory relies on our taking many other objects, such as our measuring instruments, to be where we perceptually find them.

So the third proposition fails, and its failure brings down the second with it. We have no good reason to believe that the causes of our sense-experiences are merely structural counterparts of the objects which it seems to us that we perceive, situated in a space of their own, and even if we were rationally entitled to hold this belief, it would be of no scientific consequence. For scientific theories to be verifiable, the 'minute parts', as Locke called them, on which the behaviour of physical objects is supposed to depend, must, if they are really parts of anything, be parts of objects which can be perceptually located. The theories may give us reason to conclude that these objects are in some respects very different from what they appear to us to be – this is a question which we have still to examine – but they cannot be so different as to belong to quite another spatio-temporal system. At best such merely postulated objects could serve as models, but this is not the role assigned to them in any version of the causal theory.

I may say in passing that if Russell had been right in holding what

I once called the iron-curtain theory of perception, his conclusion that everything that a man perceives is physically located in his head would not have been ridiculous. It depended on his treating what he called percepts as the contents of experiences and then anticipating current fashion by identifying these experiences with events in the brain. His mistake lay in treating percepts as initially subjective and in rejecting his earlier view that an objective spatial system can, and indeed must, be developed out of them, if it is to be developed at all. Not that his own method of achieving this was altogether satisfactory. I have tried to show elsewhere how I think that it might be done.[11]

But now what becomes of the first of our three propositions, the claim that the features of our actual sense-experiences, taken by themselves, make it probable that they have external causes? Can it survive without the other two? Not to any purpose, because it owed its content to them. The claim loses all interest, once it is admitted that the causes cannot be identified.

At this point I must try to make it clear that I am not presenting a case for scepticism. I concede that the features of our sense-experiences are such as make it both possible and useful for us to adopt what Hume called 'the common hypothesis of the identity and continuance of our interrupted perceptions'. I concede that when the development of this primitive theory has transmuted percepts into relatively stable objects, we can proceed to credit these objects with causal powers. I allow even for a sophisticated move by which the theory absorbs its origins, so that percepts come to be treated as effects of the objects which they have served to constitute. All that I am denying is that we can have any rational ground for crediting our experiences with causes which are not otherwise identified and for situating these causes in a world of their own to which our senses literally give us no access.

In his book *Problems From Locke*, J. L. Mackie appears to reject the line of argument which I have been pursuing. He questions the dogma, as he calls it, 'that causal statements can be made only if the objects taken as causes are independently identified',[12] and claims to be able to justify what, following Jonathan Bennett, he refers to as 'the veil-of-perception doctrine'.[13] The argument on which he principally relies is 'that the real existence of material things outside us is a well-confirmed outline hypothesis, that it explains the

---

[11] *Vide The Central Questions of Philosophy*, ch. V.
[12] p. 68.   [13] p. 51.

experiences we have better than any alternative hypothesis would, in particular better than the minimal hypothesis that there are just these experiences and nothing else'.[14] But what, more precisely, is this outline hypothesis and how is it confirmed? Pretty well all that Mackie tells us is that what is essential in it 'is that it fills in gaps in things as they appear, so producing continuously existing things and gradual changes where the appearances are continuous. Its resulting merit', he says, 'is a special sort of simplicity.'[15] But what has this filling in of gaps to do with the location of physical objects behind the veil of perception? As Mackie himself acknowledges, it is just the activity which Hume attributes to the imagination so as to 'give rise to the opinion of the continued existence of body' on the basis of the 'constancy' and 'coherence' of our impressions.[16] So far as this goes I do not see how Mackie's position differs from my own.

How far Mackie is from vindicating what would ordinarily be regarded as a representative theory of perception comes out quite clearly in the solitary example that he gives. He begins by explaining that 'on the kind of representative view that we are now examining, appearances are not a special kind of entity: to speak of appearances is just to speak generally of such matters as how-it-looks or how-it-feels. So,' he continues, 'what I seem to be presented with is just that when a feelable cup-shaped object comes to be before my eyes, I begin to have a certain visual sensation, and when the object is removed I cease to have it, the whole set of observations being repeatable in just the ways needed to confirm a causal relationship: I seem to be getting evidence of a real solid object causing sensations.'[17] But between what terms is the causal relationship supposed to hold? Between how-it-is and how-it-looks? And what does the 'it' refer to here? In the example, to a feelable cup-shaped object, which is noticeably removed. Not, therefore, to a Lockean or Russellian duplicate of a cup, for *ex hypothesi*, that is not feelable, nor can it be noticeably removed: we cannot equate its removal with how-it-fails-to-feel-or-look, for then the causal relation would be short of a term: we should have merely the absence of the effect with nothing to mark the absence of the cause. But to what then? What is this feelable cup-shaped object that visibly comes and goes? Nothing other than what I also take it to be: the product of a Humean transcript from the sensory scene. This is the only interpretation

[14] p. 64.   [15] Ibid.   [16] Loc. cit.   [17] Op. cit., p. 65.

that makes any sense of Mackie's example. I may remark also that his example in no way violates the rule that causal statements can be made only if the objects taken as causes are independently identified, for the cup is identified by sight and touch before any causal powers are attributed to it. It starts, if you can bear the metaphor, as a physical object cadet. Experience decides whether it qualifies for a commission. When it obtains its commission it is allowed to exercise command. The duplicate cup for which a careless reader might suppose that Mackie was arguing cannot even be mustered as a recruit.

The rejection of what I earlier called a two-world theory would not in itself prevent us from holding that things are in some ways very different from what they appear to us to be, or even from adopting something like Locke's distinction between primary and secondary qualities. Though it is most probably correct to ascribe a two-world theory to Locke himself, he sometimes writes as though he held a different view, which his commentators and the causal theorists who have followed him have usually failed to distinguish from the other. According to this second view, a physical object would not be a duplicate of the skeleton which remains when the union of the ideas of primary and secondary qualities is dissolved: it would actually be that skeleton. There would seem to be no reason, as I said before, why its genuine outline should not be thought capable of being displayed to our sense of touch, even if the scientific considerations which strip the object of its colour were also taken to show that its felt texture was part of the clothing in which we helped to deck it out. There is, indeed, the difficulty, which Mackie notices, that Locke's actual list of primary qualities is insufficient to give the object substance, since, except for solidity, they are merely geometrical; and solidity being only the power to exclude other things from the space which our object occupies, we still require something not only to exercise this power but to differentiate the object from the space. Perhaps the quality of mass would serve the purpose. As such it would not be perceptible, but this would be a fact that the theory could tolerate, since it proceeds on the principle that, with the possible exception of its tangible outline, the object appears to us only in disguise.

This theory has the merit of allowing physical objects to be literally perceptible, even if they are never perceived as they really are, and of allowing them to occupy the positions in which we actually seem to find them. Admittedly, there is something rather tricky about the manœuvre of determining the position of an object visually by means of the property of colour which it is then held not to possess, but I have not found an argument to show that it is illegitimate. It is not like the use of Wittgenstein's ladder, where we are required to accept propositions as true, which are then declared to be nonsensical.[18] There is also the consequence, which offended Berkeley, that the theory yields a physical world that cannot be pictured; but perhaps this too is tolerable. Perhaps we can conceive what we cannot imagine; or perhaps we can imagine what we cannot visualize. At any rate let us suppose that Berkeley can be overridden. The question remains why the theory should be adopted. Why should only the skeletons of the objects that we perceive be considered to be real?

The arguments which we are offered is that they fully satisfy the needs of physics. As Mackie puts it, 'Despite the change from a Newtonian to an Einsteinian space-time framework, physics still recognizes, on a large scale, countable things with at least relative positions and extensions and motions, and despite the Quantum Theory, it still recognizes, on a small scale, particles with something like these spatio-temporal determinations. Solidity, it is true, no longer plays anything like the part it played in Boyle's theory, but is replaced by electro-magnetic fields or attraction and repulsion forces; but fairly close relations of all the other Boyle–Locke primary qualities still figure among the data of physical explanation, whereas no resemblances of our ideas of secondary qualities figure among these data.'[19] And later, having raised the question 'What would be required to justify our taking colours to be primary qualities?', he takes the principal requirement to be that we should have 'a scientific case for postulating the existence of qualities with the spatial structure of colours, either in addition to or instead of the hypothesized micro-structure to which physicists would at present refer in explaining colour phenomena'.[20] In other words, if our seeing colour can be explained without our having to assume that physical objects are literally coloured, we should not make this assumption. Even if we are too cautious to infer that physical objects are not literally coloured, we can at least conclude that we have no good reason for believing that they are.

[18] *Vide* L. Wittgenstein's *Tractatus Logico-Philosophicus*, 6.54.
[19] Op. cit., p. 18.   [20] p. 19.

In trying to assess this argument there are two questions that we need to answer. In the first place, what is meant by saying that an object literally or intrinsically possesses such and such a property? These expressions are current in the literature and I have so far used them without explanation, but we shall soon see that they present quite serious difficulties. Secondly, why should the fact that a property figures in the scientific explanation of the way things appear to us be the sole justification for including it in the list of properties that physical objects literally possess? Since the answer to the second question must partly depend on the way in which the first is answered, let us begin with the first.

I take it that in the present context the words 'literally' and 'intrinsically' are treated as equivalent: it may also be said that a property does not really belong to an object unless it belongs to it literally or intrinsically. Thus, we are sometimes told that physical objects are not really coloured, when what is meant is that colour is not one of their intrinsic properties. So how are intrinsic properties distinguished? The first answer that might come to mind is that a property is intrinsic to an object if and only if the object possesses it independently of its relation to any other objects. In shorter terms, a property is to be counted as intrinsic if and only if it is not a relational property. But now it is very far from clear that this will yield the desired distinctions. An object's spatial properties are supposed to be primary, but are they not relational? Does not the ascription of mass or electric charge to a physical object involve a consideration of the way in which other things are affected by it? And conversely, is it entirely obvious that colour is a relational property? One ground for saying that it is would be that an object is coloured only in relation to light. It might, however, be argued that the dependence of colour upon light is causal rather than logical, and if causal dependence is going to count as making a property relational, it is not clear that any property is going to be intrinsic.

So let us try a different course. Perhaps the word 'literally' may prove more tractable. Suppose we were to say that a physical object literally possesses just those properties that are ascribable to it without reference to an observer. Whether we continued to use the word 'intrinsically' as equivalent to 'literally' in this context or applied it only to the possession of those properties, if there are any, which are wholly non-relational would be of no importance. Then the ground for saying that physical objects are not literally coloured would be that the ascription of colour to them is a matter of saying how they would appear to normal observers in normal circumstances. It could, indeed, be argued that this is not what ascriptions of colour are commonly taken to mean by persons unschooled in physics or philosophy, since they are more likely to view colours as intrinsic properties; but that need not concern us. It will be enough if we can agree that a reference at least to a possible observer is involved in the truth-conditions of the statements in which physical objects have colours ascribed to them.

But now the question arises whether this is a distinctive feature of colour and of the other qualities which, according to Locke, are wrongly transferred to objects from ideas. No doubt it is also a feature of sounds and tastes and smells, but does it mark them off from anything else? Are there any properties at all which can significantly be ascribed to a physical object without some reference at least to a possible observer? Let it be granted that we are entitled to credit physical objects with properties that are not straightforwardly open to observation in the way that colours are. Even so, we could not understand the statements in which such properties are ascribed unless we knew what the conditions were under which they, or at least the theories in which they figured, were to be accounted true or false; and in what could these conditions consist if not in the occurrence of states of affairs that were straightforwardly observable?

There appears to be only one way in which this objection can be met. One would have to draw a distinction between the truth-conditions of a statement and the conditions under which it is acceptable. In some cases, as, for example, in the ascription of colour to a currently existing object, these might coincide, but in others they would not. For instance, it is the existence of current records that makes a statement about the past acceptable, but its truth-condition might more plausibly be equated with the actual occurrence of the past event; or again, the view may be taken that whereas the conditions for the acceptance of a statement about the mental state of another person relates to his behaviour, its truth-condition is his actually undergoing the experience in question. Then the argument would be that this distinction applied also to statements in which physical objects were credited with mass or electric charge or any of the Lockean primary qualities. The conditions for the acceptance of any such statement would carry a reference to what might be observed, but its truth-conditions would not. They would simply consist in the object's satisfying the theoretical requirements for the possession of the property in question, independently of the experiences or even the existence of any possible observer. The totality of these properties would then be taken as furnishing us with a description of physical objects as they really are.

This position has its awkward features, even if we admit the distinction on which it rests. As we have already noted, it requires us to discount the property of colour by means of which objects are visually located, while still retaining their location, and it correspondingly yields a physical world which we are unable to picture. Nevertheless I think that it is tenable. It has the merit of giving a tolerable answer to the difficult question of the relation between the 'two worlds' of physics and common sense, and it squares with the scientific account of perception. Its advocates would, however, be mistaken if they claimed that the scientific account of perception forced it upon us. Not only are we not obliged to interpret the details of this account realistically, but even if we choose to do so, we need not draw the conclusion that the properties which serve to explain the ways in which physical objects appear to us are the only properties that they really have. It is not as if we were already furnished with a criterion of reality which the primary qualities are alone discovered to satisfy. The distinctions which we are accustomed to draw between the way objects appear and the way they really are require us only to discriminate among appearances: they permit us to say such things as that a fabric is really red but looks purple in the fading light, or that under certain conditions a fruit which is really sweet tastes sour. To assert that physical objects are not really coloured or that they are really tasteless is therefore to use the word 'really' in a different sense, for which a criterion has to be provided. In fact, what is happening in this instance is that one fixes on a particular method for picking out the primary qualities and then just chooses to say that only the qualities which are picked out by this method are really inherent in the objects that possess them. The choice is open to us, just because there is no antecedent criterion of reality with which it could conflict.

This is not, however, the only choice that we can reasonably make. It is also open to us to take the common-sense view which allows us to conceive of physical objects as persisting in much the same form as that in which they normally appear to us. As we have seen, this choice is sometimes thought to be excluded by the scientific account of perception, but I believe this to be a mistake. We need to attain the level of theory at which, as I mentioned earlier, percepts come to be dissociated from the objects which they have served to constitute. There will then be no difficulty of principle in supposing them to be systematically correlated with features of these objects and with other factors. We can even take a realistic view of scientific particles by conceiving of them as literally composing the things that we perceive. It will then follow, what Locke sometimes writes as if he held, that their being unobservable is not a matter of principle but merely due to their being so minute. Admittedly, this view also has its awkward consequences. It obliges us to hold that colour is not the dissective property that it appears to be, since we shall be crediting coloured objects with colourless parts, and that there are unperceived gaps in the minute textures of surfaces which we take to be continuous. I do not, however, consider these drawbacks to be any greater than those of the view that we previously considered. If anything, I am inclined to think them less.

The question remains whether it should be regarded as a necessary condition for an object to be perceived that there be a causal relation of the appropriate sort between the object and percipient. I have indeed argued that physical objects cannot be introduced as causes in the first instance. There is no room either for any such causal factor in the process of developing objects out of percepts or in the original assignments of their positions in space. This is, however, all at a more primitive level than that at which we introduce persons into our theory and further distinguish between their perceptions and the objects which they perceive. At the more advanced stage, where both the putative causes and their putative effects can be independently identified, there is no logical objection to our writing a causal condition into our account of perception, if we have any good reason for doing so. That we do have such reasons has been sufficiently well argued by Professor Grice. He considers a case in which a man is induced by post-hypnotic suggestion or the stimulation of his cortex to think that he sees a clock at a place where there actually happens to be one, and another case in which the operation of a looking-glass, reflecting light from a particular pillar, causes it to look as if there was a pillar at a place where a similar pillar actually stands; and he maintains, I think plausibly, that in the first case we should not say that the man saw the clock, on the ground that he would have had the same experience even if the clock had not been there, and that in the second case we should say that the man saw the pillar from which the light was reflected rather than the one that was actually at the place where a pillar looked to him to be.[21] I am not sure that the fact of our invoking causal considerations in these exceptional cases entitles us to hold that they enter into the meaning of all our perceptual statements, but I do not mind saying that they enter into their truth-conditions. The point, however, that I wish to emphasize is that this causal factor is subsidiary. The information which our judgements of perception yield us would suffer no loss if we ignored it, and it plays no part in forming our original conception of the perceptible world.

I should like to remark in conclusion that there is a parallel here between perception and memory. It has become fashionable in recent years to write a causal condition into the analysis of memory, the argument being that it is only by tracing the appropriate causal path between the event remembered and the remembering of it that we can distinguish the genuine memory of a past event from a true belief in its occurrence which is derived from some other source. It seems that the tracing of the path would have to go into scientific detail, so that it is again questionable whether the causal condition should be held to enter into the meaning of the memory statements on which it bears. Nevertheless the argument for regarding it as a truth condition is persuasive. Here too, however, it should be obvious that past events cannot be introduced as the otherwise unknown causes of our apparent memories of them. We cannot pick and choose among them in order to forge the right causal links, unless they have been independently identified. And how can this be originally achieved except through memory? The insertion of a causal clause into the analysis of some of our judgements of memory is therefore only a subsidiary refinement. It depends on our taking the experiences on which these judgements are initially based as pointing on their own to the occurrence of past events.

[21] Op. cit., p. 142.

4 *On a Supposed Antinomy*

I wish to offer a very simple solution of the logical puzzle concerning the man who was sentenced to be executed in the course of a given week, on condition that he did not know, when the day set for his execution arrived, that it was the fatal day. Arguing that he could not be executed on the seventh day, since if he survived till then he would know that this was the fatal day, and that he could not be executed on the sixth day, since, the seventh day being excluded, this became the last possible day and the same reasoning applied, and that by the same token he could not be executed on the fifth day, and so back through the week, he concluded that the sentence could not be carried out. Where, if at all, did he go wrong?

Professor Quine, in a paper which he first published in *Mind* (vol. 62, January 1953) and has reprinted in his book *The Ways of Paradox*, maintains that the man's reasoning was faulty, on the ground that the conclusion, which he finally reached, that he would not be executed was a possibility that he should have taken into account from the start. But then he would not be entitled to claim, if he survived to the seventh day, that he knew he would be executed on that day. He could claim only to know that either he would be executed on that day or not at all, and in that case it would be consistent with the data that he should be executed even on the seventh day, let alone on any of the others.

I think that Quine's argument is valid *ad hominem*, but I do not think that it gets to the root of the puzzle. Suppose that the condition were that the man should not know, on the day set for his execution, that he was to be executed on that day if he was to be executed at all, it would still appear paradoxical that he could be sure of getting off.

A slight elaboration of the story will, I think, show clearly that Quine's answer is insufficient, and also lead to the solution of the puzzle. Let us suppose that a set of seven cards, known to include the Ace of Spades, is put in the man's cell, in a place where it cannot be tampered with, and every morning the prison chaplain comes in and draws a card. On the day when the chaplain draws the Ace of Spades, the man is to die, provided that he does not know that the Ace of Spades will be drawn on that day. The man argues that the Ace of Spades cannot be the last card in the sequence, for then he would know that it was coming up, that it cannot be the sixth card either, since the elimination of the seventh card reduces the members of the sequence to six, and so on as before. Here it is irrelevant whether the drawing of the Ace of Spades is actually followed by the man's execution, or even whether the chaplain in fact remembers to come and draw the card. What the man's argument, and indeed the original puzzle, purports to show is that there cannot be an event of which it is true both that it is known to be a member of a given sequence, and that its position in the sequence is uncertain, in the sense that when one runs through the sequence one does not know at what stage in it the event will occur.

This last claim is ambiguous, and I have deliberately made it so, because it is on an ambiguity at this point that I believe the whole puzzle turns. The ambiguity is between being unable to predict *before the sequence is run through* when the event in question will occur and being unable to make this prediction *in the course of the run, however long it continues.* In the first case, there is uncertainty, but in the second there may not be. Thus if one is presented with an ordinary well-shuffled pack of cards and asked to bet once for all on the position of the Ace of Spades, the odds, unless one is gifted with extra-sensory perception, are fifty-one to one against one's being right. On the other hand, if one is allowed to continue betting as the cards are exposed, there may come a time when one is betting on a certainty, if the Ace of Spades is the last card to appear. We may concede to Quine that it is not an absolute certainty, since the pack may after all prove faulty and not contain the Ace of Spades, but this does not affect the argument. The distinction which I have made remains.

To see how this solves the puzzle, let us simplify the story by supposing that the date of the execution has been set for one of the two succeeding days. If the condition of the prisoner's escaping it is that he knows which day has been selected, he does not escape, since he does not know, though he has an even chance of correctly guessing, which day it is. But if the condition is that there could be a time at which he would know which day had been selected, he does escape, since this time would come if the execution were set for the second day. A fallacy occurs if the second case is projected on to the first and it is argued that because there could be circumstances in which all uncertainty had been removed, there is no uncertainty at the start. It is only because the two cases are not distinguished in the formulation of the puzzle that the appearance of an antinomy arises.

5 *Identity and Reference*

'Things are identical if and only if they have the same properties.'
This definition of identity stems from Leibniz and is nowadays
commonly known as Leibniz's law. Does it state both a necessary
and a sufficient condition of identity? It is at least doubtful whether
it states a sufficient condition, since it is not obvious that things are
logically incapable of being numerically different without differing
in any other respect. The question turns in part on what is allowed
to count as a property. Clearly if properties like 'being identical with
me' are admissible, it will follow trivially that no two different things
can have all the same properties. No one who is not identical with
me can be identical with me. On the other hand, if we consider only
general properties, as we must do if the question is to be of any
interest, then, as I have argued elsewhere,[1] there are grounds for
thinking that the principle of the identity of indiscernibles is not a
necessary truth. For instance, it would not be a necessary truth, if we
allowed the possibility that things which are not descriptively
distinguishable may yet be distinguished demonstratively.

This is not, however, a question that I wish to pursue here.
Instead, I shall begin by asking whether Leibniz's law states even a
necessary condition of identity. Can there be identical things which
do not have all their properties in common? This question sounds
strange, because in speaking of things in the plural we already
appear to be denying their identity. Let us therefore rephrase it in
what used to be called the formal mode. If the expressions '*a*' and '*b*'
denote the same object, can there be any predicate '*f*' such that the
sentence '*fa*' states a true proposition but the sentence '*fb*' does not?
This consorts with Leibniz's own formulation 'Eadem sunt quorum
unum potest substitui alteri salva veritate' – 'Things are the same
when one can be substituted for the other without loss of truth',

---

[1] See my article 'On the Identity of Indiscernibles', reprinted in my *Philosophical Essays*, pp. 26–35.

except that Leibniz should have talked of substituting expressions rather than the things for which the expressions stand.

At first sight it would appear obvious that the answer to our question must be 'No'. A thing has the properties that it has. How can our designating it in different ways make any difference? How can there be a property which one and the same thing possesses under one designation but not under another? Of course one and the same thing may possess different properties at different times, and we may use different designations to refer to different phases of its history. Saul was a persecutor of the Christians, Paul their champion, yet Saul and Paul were the same person. It is, however, easy to show that such cases present no serious difficulty. All we have to do is to build the temporal reference into the description of the property. Whether we call him Saul or Paul, one and the same person had the property of being a persecutor of Christians throughout such and such a period and the different but compatible property of being a champion of Christians throughout such and such a later period. This move is less easily made when the person's history is not yet complete, but it is equally valid. In one way of speaking, many things are true of a boy that will not be true of the man that he will become, and many things will be true of the man that are not now true of the boy. Even so, since the boy and the man are the same person, we can say that it is timelessly true of him both that he has the properties which consist in his having such and such characteristics at an earlier time and that he has the properties which consist in his having such and such other characteristics at a later time. Again, these properties will not be incompatible when the time-references are included in their description. We may not yet know what many of these later properties are, but this is no bar to his timelessly possessing them.

There is no great difficulty either about the cases, whether real or fictional, in which the different designations refer not to different phases of a person's history but to different aspects of his character. In Robert Louis Stevenson's story of Dr Jekyll and Mr Hyde, one and the same person is credited with two very different personalities. The effect is heightened by his being given a different appearance when the bad personality is dominant, as well as a different name. The disparity, however, differs only in degree from that which we often find between Philip drunk and Philip sober; if this is not thought to pose any problem of identity it is because people remain recognizable in their cups and while they may be subject to different epithets they are not commonly known by different names. Even so, the cases are parallel. Just as Philip has the properties of behaving in such and such ways when he is drunk, and in such and such different ways when he is sober, so Stevenson's hero, by whatever name we call him, is represented as behaving in a fiendish way when he is under the influence of the drug and in a benevolent way when he is not. It sounds odd to say that Mr Hyde is portrayed as being a good man under any conditions because the use of the name 'Mr Hyde' carries the implication that the prevalent conditions are those in which the bad behaviour comes to the fore, but if the name is taken simply to refer to the protagonist of the story, then it is true that Mr Hyde is portrayed as being in the main a good man and equally true that Dr Jekyll is portrayed as being on occasion a villain.

Nevertheless, there notoriously are properties that do at least appear to characterize an object under one designation but not under another. Or rather, since there may be a question whether these ought to count as properties, let us say that there appear to be predicates which an object may or may not satisfy according as it is differently designated. These predicates belong to three main groups. There are those in which use is made of modal terms, as when it is said that something is necessarily such and such, there are those which contain a reference to propositional attitudes, like doubting or believing, and there are those containing verbs like 'admiring' or 'seeking' to which the assignment of the right accusatives depends upon the subject's beliefs. For example, it may be true that Mr Smith, the bank manager, is generally admired, but false that the local peeping-Tom is generally admired: yet, unknown to his fellow-citizens, Mr Smith *is* the local peeping-Tom. Similarly, someone may not know that Cecil Day-Lewis wrote any fiction, while knowing that Nicholas Blake was a writer of detective stories. Since these are different names of the same person, it appears to follow that the predicate of being known by so and so to have written fiction is satisfied by the former Poet Laureate under one designation but not under another. As for modal predicates, we need look no further than Quine's well-known example of the number of the planets. The numeral '9' and the expression 'the number of the planets' denote the same number. Yet while the proposition that 9 is necessarily greater than 4 is generally thought to be true, the proposition that the number of planets is necessarily greater than 4 appears to be false. It is surely a contingent fact that there are just so many planets, and not at least five fewer.

It is to be remarked that all these examples can be construed in ways that do not lead to paradox. In the case of the number of the planets, we have to distinguish the true proposition 'There is a number such that it is both the number of the planets and can be designated in a way from which it necessarily follows that it is greater than 4' from the false proposition 'There is a number such that it necessarily is both the number of the planets and can be designated in a way from which it follows that it is greater than 4.' The sentence 'The number of the planets is necessarily greater than 4' is open to either interpretation, and because of this ambiguity it is also an ambiguous question whether the predicate of being necessarily greater than 4 is satisfied by the object which is indifferently designated by the numeral '9' and by the expression 'the number of the planets'. If the object is designated by the numeral '9' it does satisfy this predicate, if it is referred to simply as 'the number of the planets', it does not. But surely, it will be objected, these are not two different objects: they are one and the same. And how can one and the same object both satisfy and fail to satisfy the same predicate? The answer to this, as we shall see, is that objects do not have necessary properties except in virtue of the way that we describe them. To say that an object satisfies the predicate of being necessarily so and so is just to say that 'being so and so' is a necessary consequence of some predicate which it satisfies. So 'being greater than 4' is logically comprised in 'being the number 9' but not logically comprised in 'being the number of the planets'. But then the puzzle vanishes. There is nothing odd about the fact that different descriptions carry different implications, whether or not the same object satisfies them.

A similar ambiguity occurs in our other example. The sentence 'The local peeping-Tom is generally admired' expresses a true proposition, or at least one that so passes in our story, if it is taken to mean that there is someone who is both the local peeping-Tom and is generally admired; for our Mr Smith is supposed to satisfy both these predicates. The same sentence might, however, more naturally be taken to mean that the activities of the local peeping-Tom were generally admired, with the implication that he would be admired for them whoever he turned out to be, and this we are supposing to be false. So if we were to ask the citizens 'Do you admire the local peeping-Tom?', there is more than one way in which this question could be understood. They might take us to be asking 'Do you admire the man who is in fact the local peeping-Tom?' and in that case their answer should be 'We do not know whether we admire him or not, since we have not yet discovered who he is.' Or, again more naturally, they might take the question to be 'Do you admire the local peeping-Tom for his activities, whoever he may turn out to be?' and in that case their answer should be 'No we do not.' In this case, however, the discovery of the ambiguity fails to remove the problem, since we are still left with the conclusion that one and the same person, Mr Smith, both does and does not satisfy the predicate of being generally admired, according as he is differently designated. The reason for this is that predicates like 'being admired' apply to people only in consequence of the other descriptions which we believe them to satisfy, and these other descriptions may not always be sufficient to enable us to identify the persons who satisfy them as being one and the same. There is also the complication that the objects of such attitudes may not exist at all, as when a girl longs vainly for Mr Right. A possible move, therefore, would be to credit them with what are called 'intentional objects' to which a real object may or may not correspond. If we dealt in this way with our example, we should have to say that the attributes of being admired and despised were not attached to the person Mr Smith but to the intentional objects 'the local bank manager' and 'the local peeping-Tom'. The predicate which Mr Smith would satisfy would be that of corresponding to both these intentional objects, which raises no problem about his identity. This is in line with Frege's doctrine of sense and reference, according to which, if I understand it rightly, a sentence like 'Mr Smith is rich' refers to Mr Smith, whereas a sentence like 'Mr Smith is admired' refers not to Mr Smith, but to the sense of the name 'Mr Smith': so that in the second case Mr Smith is featured only indirectly, as being the person to whom the sense of the name refers in its turn.

These devices do remove the problem about identity, but at a good deal of a cost. Whether we speak of intentional objects or of the senses of nominative expressions, we are in either case saddled with very dubious entities. If senses are objects, as they have to be for Frege, it is not clear how they can have any reference: surely it is only signs that can be taken to refer beyond themselves. Neither is it clear, on the other view, what the relation of correspondence between Mr Smith and the intentional object 'the local bank manager' can be supposed to be, if it is not a case of identity. We might, therefore, do better to attack the problem in another way by breaking down such predicates as 'being admired' into the elements which justify their application. The fact that Mr Smith is generally admired will then be represented as consisting partly in the relations which his fellow-citizens bear to Mr Smith, their bowing to him when they meet him and so forth, and partly in the character of some of the sentences to which they assent, as for example the sentence 'Mr Smith is a good man'. The fact that the local peeping-Tom is generally despised will, in our example, consist only in the citizens' use and acceptance of such sentences as 'Such men are a disgrace to the community'. The crucial point now is that we do not proceed to analyse these sentences independently, in terms of the reference of the names or descriptions which they contain. Instead, we try to show what the citizens' acceptance of them comes to, in terms of the other sentences which they are disposed to accept or reject, and eventually in terms of the actions which they are disposed to take. One result of this will be that being spoken of in such and such a way will not be a property of Mr Smith, though it will be a property of the citizens that they make such and such uses of the name. The properties which will be assignable to Mr Smith will be properties, like those of being a bank manager, or a peeping-Tom, which he retains under any designation.

If this approach is successful, it enables us to deal also with our other example. Here again there is an ambiguity, inasmuch as the statement that the former Poet Laureate is not known to Mr A to have written fiction is false in the sense that Mr A identifies as a writer of fiction someone who is in fact the former Poet Laureate, but true in the sense that he does not so identify him *as* the Poet Laureate. And again the detection of this ambiguity does not remove the problem, since we still appear to be left with the conclusion that one and the same person, Cecil Day-Lewis, both does and does not satisfy the predicate of being known to Mr A to have written fiction, according as he is differently designated. On the view which I am advocating, however, there will be no such predicate. It will be a fact about Mr A that he assents to or dissents from a number of sentences which include the names 'Cecil Day-Lewis' and 'Nicholas Blake'. What this amounts to will again be explained in terms of his disposition to assent to or dissent from such and such other sentences, and to act in such and such ways. Since we are speaking of his knowledge we shall also be committed to the truth of the propositions which some of the sentences express. For instance, it will be held true both that Cecil Day-Lewis wrote detective stories and that Nicholas Blake wrote poetry. It makes no difference here, any more than it did in the Jekyll and Hyde example, that the names which are used in these statements are coupled in each case with the wrong activity, that is, the activity with which their bearer is usually associated under the other name. The properties which we are allowing him will accrue to him under any name to which he answers, as well as under any description which he actually satisfies.

I am aware that this is only the outline of a solution to our difficulty. To fill it in, we need to be able to show in detail how the meanings which are given to sentences can be analysed in terms of their links with other sentences, the dispositions to actions to which their acceptance gives rise, and the stimuli which evoke them, without our being obliged to have recourse to intentional objects. I made some attempt to do this in my book *The Origins of Pragmatism*, but am not wholly satisfied with the result. I therefore do not exclude the possibility of our having to be content, at least for the present, with some theory of a Fregean type, while still feeling that a better solution ought to be available.

I want now to return to the subject of modal predicates, both because it will take us a little deeper into the topic of identity and because I expect it to throw light on some vexed questions concerning our use of proper names. It is generally held to be true not only that everything has the property of being identical with itself but that this is a necessary property. In other words, it is thought to be necessarily true that for all x, $x = x$. But now, if we accept Leibniz's law, we have to allow that if y is identical with x, y has all the same properties as x. So if being necessarily identical with x is a property of x, it must also be a property of y, so long as x and y are identical. And then it will follow that every statement of identity is necessarily true, if it is true at all.

This is a very remarkable conclusion and one that many of us will be inclined to dismiss out of hand as evidently false. Yet it has its defenders. They will admit that it can be a contingent fact that one and the same object satisfies different descriptions, so that if a statement like 'The author of *David Copperfield* is identical with the author of *Sketches by Boz*' is interpreted as saying no more than that the same person wrote both books, it is allowed to be only contingently true. On the other hand, if we replace the phrase 'the author of *David Copperfield*' by the name 'Charles Dickens' and the phrase 'the author of *Sketches by Boz*' by the name 'Boz' and so find ourselves asserting that Dickens is Boz, we shall be told that we are now expressing a necessarily true proposition. The reason which is alleged for this change is that whereas different descriptions which are satisfied by the same object can have different senses, thus allowing the fact that they are so satisfied to be contingent, the same does not apply to proper names. On this view, the sense of a proper name just consists in its denoting the object that it does. Consequently, two names which denote the same object will have the same sense. But if they do have the same sense is it not possible that they denote different objects? It follows that if any sentence of the form '$a = b$', where 'a' and 'b' are proper names, expresses a true proposition, it expresses a proposition which is necessarily true.

One obvious objection to this conclusion is that the truth of such propositions cannot be determined *a priori*. We need to know some literary history in order to be able to identify Boz with Dickens. That Hesperus, the so-called evening star, is identical with Phosphorus, the so-called morning star, and identical also with the planet Venus was an astronomical discovery. It is a historical fact that the Roman Camulodunum is identical with the English Colchester. Though it happens that all these propositions are very well established, it is certainly not unthinkable that any one of them should turn out to be false.

The reply which is made to this objection, for example by Professor Kripke, in his paper 'Naming and Necessity',[2] is that it is a mistake to assume that if a proposition is necessarily true, it must also be true *a priori*. To say that a proposition is necessarily true is to say that it could not have been otherwise, that it would remain true in any possible world. To say that a proposition is true *a priori* is to say that it can be known to be true, at any rate of this world, independently of all experience. But then, Kripke argues, it is by no means obvious that propositions which are necessarily true, in the sense defined, must also be such as to be capable of being known to be true independently of experience. He cites as a counterexample Goldbach's conjecture that every even number is the sum of two primes. Since

[2] Published in *Semantics of Natural Language*, edited by Donald Davidson and Gilbert Harman.

this is a proposition in pure mathematics, it may be taken to be necessarily true, if it is true at all: if it is not necessarily true, its negation is. Yet it can hardly be thought capable of being known either to be true or to be false independently of experience, since for all the work that has been done on it, nobody has so far succeeded either in demonstrating it or in finding an exception to it.

But if this is to pass as a counterexample to the thesis that necessary propositions are *a priori*, propositions which do qualify as *a priori* are going to be hard to find. Learning the meaning of logical and mathematical signs presumably counts as an experience, and so does going through a proof: and while it may not be unthinkable that people should come to know mathematical truths without having had these experiences, one can confidently say that it never actually happens. One might try to make the concept of the *a priori* a little more serviceable by ruling that a proposition is to be accounted *a priori* if some people are able to discover its truth merely through understanding the meaning of the signs which express it. This would have the odd consequence, for those who think like Kripke, that statements of identity such as 'Dickens is Boz' turn out to be *a priori* as well as necessary, in consequence of the equation of understanding the sense of a proper name with knowing what object it denotes. On the other hand, many of the propositions which commonly pass for *a priori* truths would still not qualify, if their truth is not evident until one has gone through the proof. Would children be able to grasp even the simplest mathematical propositions, if they did not have the experience of assembling objects and counting them? Perhaps some of them would, but if this is what it comes down to, the concept of the *a priori* is not only uncertain in its application but of very little interest. In fact, it has not traditionally been linked with questions of child psychology. What has been thought to be at issue has been not so much the ways in which propositions can be learned as the ways in which they acquire their truth-values. To characterize them as *a priori* is here to imply that their truth or falsehood can be established on purely logical or semantic grounds, with the consequence that they are not subject to the jurisdiction of empirical fact. But then there is no difference between saying of a proposition that it is true *a priori* and saying that it is true because it is logically or semantically necessary.

This brings us back to the question whether a statement of identity can be semantically necessary in any more interesting sense than that it expresses a definition or a decision to use one name as a substitute for another. Let us look at the examples which Kripke gives. One of them is the proposition that heat is the motion of molecules. Kripke admits that this proposition came to be accepted only as the result of scientific enquiry, and he also allows it to be possible both that the molecular motion in question should not have given rise to our sensations of heat and that something else should have. What he infers from this, however, is not that heat is not necessarily the motion of molecules, but that heat does not necessarily produce sensations of heat. We can imagine Martians coming to earth and having, under these conditions, sensations not of heat but of cold. We would say they felt heat as cold. And why should the same not have been true of ourselves?

This is all very well, but suppose that the molecular motion in which we take heat to consist did not have the effect of raising temperature, that it did not cause anything to burn, that it was not transformable into energy, should we still wish to say that it was heat? What Kripke has done is to detach just one of the properties which are associated with the word 'heat' from the rest of the group and argue that it is not essential. So long as he kept the others constant, he might have done the same with any other single property. This does not in the least prove that the equation with molecular motion *is* essential, any more than the effect of raising temperature, which appears to me to be a stronger candidate. Of course one can arbitrarily decide to use the word 'heat' to refer to such and such motions of molecules, no matter what their effects, but it *would* be an arbitrary decision and to my mind a silly one. If, as is logically possible, it were empirically discovered that this molecular motion had none of the effects that we associate with heat, should we really be willing to say that we had been mistaken in supposing that heat had any of these effects? Should we not rather take the mistake to have been in identifying heat with molecular motion? Indeed, one may well ask what can be meant by saying that they are identical if it is not just a way of expressing the contingent proposition that molecular motion of such and such a sort does have such and such a collection of effects.

A similar perversity is shown in Kripke's defence of his contention that light is necessarily a stream of photons. He says that we could imagine that the planet was inhabited by creatures who got visual instead of auditory sensations when there were sound waves in the air, but that we should not then say that under these circumstances sound would have been light. We should say rather that these creatures were visually sensitive to sound. But what, one may ask, is the point of talking about sound-waves, if there is no implication that they have audible effects? One might indeed imagine their being visually detectable, while retaining their other properties; one might imagine even that there were some creatures in which they aroused only visual sensations, so long as this was not true in general: but if waves of the character in question were to produce all the effects that are now ascribed to the particles with which we identify light, and vice versa, then the natural thing to say would be not that the behaviour of sound and light had been reversed but that our identification had been wrong. The waves which we had wrongly thought to be productive of sound were productive of light and the particles in which we had mistakenly supposed light to consist had been found to act in ways that were characteristic not of light but of sound. Once more the cash-value of the statement that light is a stream of photons is the contingent proposition that photons have such and such effects. If this turned out to be false, there would be no point in maintaining the identification. It is, indeed, always open to us to emulate Humpty-Dumpty, but apart from amusing ourselves in this way, it is hard to see what reason we could have for severing the concept of light from nearly all the phenomena with which it has been associated.

We come next to Hesperus and Phosphorus. Kripke denies that we can imagine circumstances in which they would not have have been identical. He allows it to be conceivable that while Venus was still to be found at its usual place in the morning, the position which it occupied in the evening might instead have been occupied by Mars, and he admits that in that case we should probably have a different use for the names 'Hesperus' and 'Phosphorus'. We should still use 'Phosphorus' to refer to Venus but 'Hesperus' would be understood to refer to Mars. He argues, however, that this does not prove that Hesperus might not have been Phosphorus, as these names are actually used. All that it proves is that the planet Venus which they both actually designate might conceivably have followed a different trajectory. But this argument is surely disingenuous. Of course if we use the names 'Hesperus' and 'Phosphorus' simply as substitutes for 'Venus' it is going to be hard to attach a sense to saying that Hesperus and Phosphorus might not have been

identical, for what we should then be saying is that Venus might not
have been Venus. I shall argue later on that the interpretation of
sentences like 'Venus is Venus' is a more complicated matter than
one might suppose, but that is not the point at issue here. For clearly
no one who takes the fact that Hesperus is Phosphorus to be
contingent can be using these names simply as substitutes for
'Venus'. Neither can this have been their original use, if the identity
of Hesperus and Phosphorus required empirical discovery. The
discovery that Venus is Venus would not have needed a great deal of
astronomical research. What it did need research to establish was
the fact that the celestial body which is visible at such and such a
place in the evening is spatio-temporally continuous with the
celestial body which is visible at such and such a place in the
morning; and it is this plainly contingent fact that the sentence
'Hesperus is identical with Phosphorus' is commonly understood to
state. The cash-value of the statement of identity is contained in the
contingent proposition that two different states of affairs are related
to one another in a way that is sufficient to make them elements in
the history of one and the same object.

An example of a different kind is that of a lectern which is
supposed to be made of wood. The question is raised whether it
could have been made of ice and the answer given is that it could not
have been, not on the ground that ice is not a suitable material for
construcing lecterns, but on the ground that any lectern that was
made of ice would not have been *this* lectern. This lectern could
perhaps turn into ice or at least it could be argued that the bar to its
doing so was physical and not logical, but to suppose that it could
have been made of ice from the start, if it is in fact made of wood,
would be to sacrifice its identity.

This example is more difficult to handle, because of the obscurity
of the question what makes this lectern the particular lectern that it
is. We can give at least a rough description of the properties that
anything must have in order to belong to the class of lecterns, but
when we ask what properties, if any, essentially distinguish this
lectern from any other, we find the question puzzling. We do,
indeed, have to allow the object some latitude. Otherwise we shall
fall into the error which Moore held to be responsible for the strange
idealist view that all relations are internal to their terms: the error of
confusing the true proposition that necessarily if x has the property
P, anything that lacks P is in fact different from x with the generally

false proposition that if x in fact has P, then necessarily anything that lacks P is different from x. It is necessarily true that anything which is not in the place where this lectern is is not this lectern, but it is false that since this lectern is in this place, its being there is necessary to its identity. We have no reason to deny that it could have been elsewhere, a few feet to the left perhaps or even in another room. This is only one of the many counterfactual hypotheses about this lectern that we seem able to frame without falling into contradiction. The problem is where to draw the line.

The answer is, I believe, that we can consistently suppose anything whatsoever to be true of the lectern, subject to three limiting conditions. One of them is that we do not make it the subject of incompatible predicates; another is that if we have committed ourselves to its being a lectern we do not credit it with properties which would deny it membership of this class; and the third, and for our present purposes the most important, is that we retain some foothold in its actual history. Thus, if we start by speaking simply of 'this lectern' we cannot consistently suppose that it has not yet come into existence, or that it has traversed a path in space which does not intersect with its actual path at any single point, but we can make sense of the hypothesis that having been manufactured when and where it was it had from then on an entirely different career, and we can equally well suppose that it came to this place by an entirely different route, including a different starting-point. If we identified the lectern by some conspicuous event in its history, such as its being the lectern at which such and such an address was given, then we could imagine anything to be true of it which is consistent with its playing its part in this event; we could even allow it a complete spatio-temporal displacement, to the extent that the event in question could itself be imaginatively displaced. Again, if it were known to us as a particular work of art, we could make mistakes, or frame counterfactual hypotheses about its spatio-temporal location, without prejudice to its identity, so long as we held fast to its distinctive appearance. How far such hypotheses can go would seem to depend upon the extent of our knowledge. For example, one might be inclined to deny that the Parthenon could have been built in the eighteenth century. No doubt a building exactly resembling the Parthenon in appearance could have been built in the eighteenth century, but still, one might want to argue, to think of it as being the Parthenon, even in a counterfactual hypothesis, would be to remove the Parthenon too far from its temporal and cultural setting. On the other hand, if a schoolboy were to believe that the Parthenon was built in the eighteenth century or even that it was located in Rome rather than in Athens, should we be bound to hold that he was contradicting himself, or that he was not referring to the Parthenon? Could we not conclude that he was making a factual mistake? There just is no rule for deciding such questions. It does seem, however, that if there is any link at all to fix the reference we are disposed to treat even the wildest errors as factual, whereas we are rather more restrictive in our admission of counterfactual hypotheses.

One point which is clear is that there is no essential way of identifying any particular object. If we identify this lectern by its actual origin, we can think of it as occupying a different position at the present time: if we identify it as the lectern which is now in this position, we can think of it as having had a different origin. The result is that all propositions about this lectern, except those that are entailed by its being a lectern of any sort at all, and trivial propositions like 'This lectern is this one', can be treated as contingent. This applies just as much to propositions about the materials of which it is made as to any of the rest. We can, indeed, identify this lectern not just as being made of wood, since this will not distinguish it from other lecterns, but as being made of such and such particular pieces of wood at such and such a place and time, and then go on to frame counterfactual hypotheses about its history. But equally we can identify it by its present position and frame counterfactual hypotheses about its manufacture. It would be absurd to suppose that someone who believed that it was made of beechwood when it was in fact made of oak, or that it was made in Mr Robinson's workshop, when it was in fact made in Mr Brown's, would be holding a self-contradictory belief, or that he would not be referring to the lectern at all; and exactly the same would apply to the more wayward belief that the lectern was made of ice, if it is not a contradiction to suppose that any lectern can be made of ice. Of course if it were made of ice it would be a different lectern, in the sense that something would be true of it that actually is not, but in this sense, it would equally be a different lectern if these sheets of paper had not been placed on it, or if it had been moved into the room five minutes earlier than it actually was. One might say that its being made of wood was a more 'intimate' property of the lectern than the others that I have mentioned. It would, for example, be more likely to figure in a description of the object in an auctioneer's catalogue. On the other hand, if the sheets of paper were something like the Gettysburg address, its relation to them might figure more prominently. If the lectern had been turned into a booby trap and we were looking for those responsible, the time at which it was moved into the room might be of greater interest. And in any case none of this makes the lectern's possession of any one of these properties cease to be contingent.

I believe that very much the same applies to the identification of objects which are denoted by proper names. If the use of the proper name is to convey any information, the name must be associated with some discernible feature which is believed or imagined to belong to the object in question. In the case where such a description individuates the object, it will not be essential. Some other description would have served as well. Again the result is that the sentences in which a proper name is coupled with a description of this sort never express necessary propositions.

In saying this, I am rejecting the view, which I mentioned earlier, that the sense of a proper name consists simply in its denoting the object that it does. At first sight, the simplicity of this view might make it seem attractive. As Kripke puts it, why should we not stipulate that a name is to be taken as referring to such and such a particular object, in the same way as we stipulate that an adjectival sign is to be taken as referring to such and such a quality? If the English word 'red' can stand without further ado for the colour red, why should not the name 'Richard Nixon' stand in the same straightforward fashion for Richard Nixon? But now we must consider what is implied by saying on the one hand that an adjective stands for such and such a quality and on the other that a name denotes such and such a person. For this information to be of any use to us, we have to be able to identify the signs in question, and also to identify what they are supposed to stand for. In the first case, this presents no problem. We can recognize instances of the word 'red' and we can recognize instances of the colour red. We can also recognize instances of the name 'Richard Nixon'. But when it comes to the man Richard Nixon, the thirty-seventh President of the United States, whom we are taking the name to denote, how are we to identify him except as a man of whom such and such things are true, a man who has such and such a characteristic appearance, or

such and such a chequered history? If we set aside every description
of this sort, what are we left with? An individual substance? A bare
particular? But if that is what we take the name to denote, its use
commits us to nothing at all, since a bare particular could have any
properties whatsoever. Even if it be presupposed that the name
refers in this instance to a person, this person has to be distinguished
from all the rest; and how is this to be effected except by
distinguishing between different sets of properties? Demonstratively,
perhaps. But then the question arises what we are pointing at.
Surely not at a bare particular. At Mr Nixon. But what is Mr Nixon?
Among other things, the thirty-seventh President of the United
States.

But surely it is not necessary that he should have become
President. It was logically, even if not politically possible that he
should have been defeated in either or both of the two presidential
elections that he won. He might, indeed, never have gone into
politics at all. He might have died in infancy. Where then do we
draw the line? The answer is the same as in the case of the lectern.
We must not credit the object to which the name refers with
incompatible properties. Since anyone who failed to take the name
to refer to a person would be misunderstanding our use of it, we
must assign to its bearer whatever properties are entailed by being a
person. Beyond that we can suppose anything whatsoever to be true
of it, so long as we retain some foothold in Mr Nixon's actual
history. If we hold fast to his origin we can take liberties with the
remainder of the story, making it, indeed, as short as we please; if we
identify him by his present position we can imagine his having
reached it from a different starting-point and by a different route. If
we associate him with some conspicuous event we can displace him
in space or time, to the extent that this event itself can be displaced
without ceasing to be captured by our description of it. It is more
difficult to assimilate him to a work of art, but even here the parallel
holds. For instance, someone who thought that Goliath was not a
Philistine but a Samaritan and also located him in the wrong
century might still be held to have made only a factual mistake; we
are not bound to conclude, and probably should not conclude that
he has failed to identify Goliath, so long as he gives some description
that we find acceptable.

Are we to say then that the sense of a proper name consists in one
or more of the descriptions which the users of the name associate

with it? The objection to saying this is that it suggests that the name is shorthand for the descriptions, which it is not. It is proved not to be by the fact, which we have already noted, that the coupling of the name with any one of the descriptions, or even with all of them, yields a synthetic and not an analytic proposition. This applies even in the case where the user of the name knows nothing about the object which he intends it to denote except that such and such a description applies to it. For example, someone who associates Petra only with the line 'a rose-red city, half as old as time' can entertain the hypothesis that Petra is not rose-red in colour or that it is not a very old city. That is to say, he is not committed to regarding these propositions as self-contradictory. The reason for this, as Mr J. E. Altham has pointed out,[3] is that he knows that the object which he intends the name to denote must be capable of being identified in many other ways than that in which he identifies it, and he thinks of the name as being sustained in its reference by one of these other descriptions, even though he is not himself in a position to supply them. So when he admits the possibility that Petra is not old or not rose-red, he may suppose it to be identified by its location, whether or not he knows what this is. All that he needs is the knowledge that it can be so identified.

But if the sense of a proper name does not consist in its denoting the object that it does, and if it is not equivalent to the sense of the descriptions with which the users of the name associate it, what does it consist in? Are we to say that proper names have no sense? This too would be misleading, in that it might suggest the evidently false conclusion that the proper names do not contribute anything to the meaning of the sentences into which they enter. Nevertheless it is correct, in so far as it makes the point that to ask for the sense of a proper name invites an answer of a different sort from that which we expect when we ask for the sense of a predicate. The sense of a predicate is given by listing some other predicate, or set of predicates, to which it is equivalent; the nearest we can come to giving the sense of a proper name is by supplying some identification of the object to which it is intended to refer. Thus, if we are to attach any meaning to the question 'What is the sense of the name "Richard Nixon"?', we must regard it simply as a way of asking 'Who, or what is Richard Nixon?' and to this question any answer

[3] See the Symposium 'The Causal Theory of Names', *Proceedings of the Aristotelian Society*, Supplementary Volume XLV (1973).

will be acceptable which enables the questioner to distinguish the object that we have in mind, whether the answer takes the form of supplying another name, or, as is much more commonly the case, of supplying a predicate which the object satisfies. The proposition which is expressed by coupling the name with such a predicate will never be necessary, for the reason, which I have already given, that the predicate will only be one among indefinitely many that could serve the same purpose, and I shall show, in a moment, that the same conclusion holds when the answer takes the form of supplying another name.

It can happen that an object is most commonly identified by a description which it actualy fails to satisfy. For instance, nearly everybody who was able to give a confident answer to the question 'Who was Goliath?' would say that he was the giant Philistine whom David killed with a stone cast from a sling. I have, however, learned from Mr Gareth Evans that biblical scholars now favour the version of the story in which Goliath is killed, not by David but by Elhanan the Bethlehemite.[4] Let us suppose that we accept this version. Will the result be that the name 'Goliath' acquires a different denotation for us, since we no longer take it to refer to the Philistine champion whom David killed? Or should we rather say that the name was still used to refer to the same person, the only difference being that we had changed our belief about the way in which he met his death? If the second course recommends itself more strongly it is, I think, because Goliath is sufficiently identified for us as the giant Philistine champion. If we learned that David did kill such a giant, although he was not called by the name which we transliterate as 'Goliath', whereas the man killed by Elhanan was a nondescript Philistine soldier who happened to bear the name, then I should be inclined to say not that our belief that David killed Goliath had turned out to be false, but rather that our use of the name 'Goliath' had turned out to be idiosyncratic. We should be in the position of Warden Spooner who is reported once at the conclusion of a sermon to have returned to the pulpit and announced 'Throughout my sermon, whenever I said "Aristotle" I was of course referring to St Paul.'

A fictitious example of a similar kind which Evans borrowed from Kripke[5] consists in the supposition that the proof of the incompleteness of arithmetic, for which Professor Gödel is deservedly famous,

---

[4] In his contribution to the symposium referred to in fn. 3.   [5] Ibid.

was not in fact devised by Gödel but by an unknown Viennese of the name of Schmidt. The question then is whether those who associate the name 'Gödel' only with the description 'the man who proved the incompleteness of arithmetic' would be using the name unknowingly to refer to Schmidt. Both Evans and Kripke take it to be obvious that they would not, but I do not find it obvious at all. It seems to me rather to depend upon the way in which the story is developed. If the fraud came to light, they would most probably not draw the conclusion that they had been using the name 'Gödel' to refer to Schmidt. Identifying Gödel, as it were retrospectively, by what they had come to learn about him, they would say that they had been mistaken in attributing to him an achievement for which the credit was not his. On the other hand, if both men remained otherwise unknown, and Schmidt went to a mathematical congress, and heard people praising the subtlety of the proof and wondering who Gödel was and why they knew nothing more about him, it would be perfectly proper for him to say 'Little do they know it, but they are talking about me'. If they said to him 'So *you* are Gödel', he could truly reply 'Well, that is not in fact my name, but I am the person you were talking about'.

But how is this to be reconciled with the fact that even for those people the proposition that Gödel proved the incompleteness of arithmetic would not be pleonastic? The answer is that they can always make sense of a story like Kripke's. They can imagine themselves acquiring other means of identifying a man whom they then discover to have deceived them in claiming to satisfy the description by which they believed themselves to know him. If they are just told 'Gödel did not prove the incompleteness of arithmetic' and no more, then in default of any further explanation, all that they actually learn is that they have been calling the author of this proof by the wrong name. They can, however, assume that some further explanation is available. In the same way, so long as they go on believing that Gödel did devise the proof, they can easily allow that he might not have. Their reliance on this description 'poses' a person for them who is known to be identifiable in other ways and is therefore not confined to that pose.

We are now in a position to account for the fact that sentences of the form '*A* is *B*', where '*A*' and '*B*' are proper names, are almost invariably used to express contingent and not necessary propositions. The explanation is very simple. For there to be any point in making identity-statements of this sort, it has to be assumed that those for whom the information is intended either possess answers to only one of the questions 'Who or what is A?' and 'Who or what is B?', or possess answers to both of them, but largely different answers. Let us suppose in the first case that I do not know who or what A is, but do know who or what B is. Then my learning that A is B puts me in a position to apply any description which I have discovered to be associated with the name 'A' to the object which I have already identified under 'B'. In the second case, I learn that the object which I have identified under either heading incorporates the features of that which I have identified under the other. Thus, if I know something about Cicero but am too little of a Latinist to associate any predicate with the name 'Tully', then in learning that Tully is Cicero, I learn in the first instance only that Cicero is sometimes known by another name, but I am also put in a position to add any information I may receive about Tully to my biography of Cicero. If I know something about Dickens and have at least heard of *Sketches by Boz*, my learning that Dickens is Boz informs me that he is also the author of that work.

The same can apply when the same name occurs on either side of the identity-sign. Thus, one of Trollope's best novels bears the title *Is he Popenjoy?* The conclusion which is reached after several hundred pages is that most probably Popenjoy *is* Popenjoy. Obviously this is not the conclusion that Popenjoy, whoever he may be, is identical with himself, but rather the conclusion that the child who has been passing as Lord Popenjoy most probably is the legitimate heir to the earldom and the estates, a contingent question of a kind which arises not only in fiction. A sentence like 'Popenjoy is Popenjoy' might indeed be used to express the trivially necessary proposition that some person is who he is, but it is difficult to think of contexts in which there would be any use for such a proposition, except perhaps as an example in a treatise on formal logic.

Are we to say, then, that 'Popenjoy is Popenjoy', in the sense in which it expresses a contingent proposition, simply means that such and such a child is the legitimate heir? Does 'Dickens is Boz' just mean that one and the same person wrote such and such a book among others? Clearly not. But then what do these sentences mean? I think that this is a badly formulated question, because it implies that proper names have a meaning in a way that they do not. Just as the names 'Dickens' and 'Boz' have no determinate sense, so the sentence 'Dickens is Boz' has no standard meaning. What proposition it is understood to express on any given occasion will depend upon the answers which its interpreter has for the questions Who is Dickens? and Who is Boz? The information he receives will then be that one and the same person satisfies the whole range of predicates which these answers embody. To say that sentences like 'Dickens is Boz' express contingent propositions thus turns out to be a loose way of saying that the normal use of such sentences is to convey contingent information of this sort.

What then becomes of the argument that since being necessarily identical with x is a property of x, it must also be a property of y, if x and y are identical? Since the conclusion that identity-statements of the form 'x is y' are always necessary is false, and since this conclusion follows from the premisses of the argument, at least one of the premisses must be false. Either it is not true that if x and y are identical, x and y have the same properties, or it is not true that being necessarily identical with x is a property of x. Strange as it may sound, I believe that the second of these propositions is the one that is false. I deny that being necessarily identical with x is a property of x, because I deny that there is any such property as that of being necessarily identical with x. It is of course true that things are identical with themselves, if this is just a way of saying that things are what they are, or that they have whatever properties they have. If we permit ourselves to quantify over properties we can allow that the formula 'for all x, for all f, fx if and only if fx' expresses a true proposition: we can allow even that in substitution instances such as 'fa if and only if fa' express necessarily true propositions, provided that the sign 'a' in each of its occurrences is used not only with the same reference but in association with exactly the same answer to the question 'Who or what is a?'. This is, however, quite a strong proviso, and the fact that we need to make it explains why true propositions which are expressed by sentences of the form 'fa if and only if fb' will seldom be necessarily true. The reason then why there is no such property as being necessarily identical with x is that to say that a property necessarily characterizes such and such an object is just a way of saying that some sentence which serves to predicate the property of the object expresses a necessary proposition; and whether this is so or not depends upon the way in which the object is designated. So no matter whether 'a' and 'b' are names or descriptions, the sentence 'a is identical with b' will express a true proposition so long as '*a*' and '*b*' have the same reference, but the sentence '*a* is necessarily identical with *b*' will express a true proposition only if the propositions which are expressed by the sentences '*fa*' and '*fb*' whatever predicate '*f*' may be, are also logically equivalent, which will very seldom be the case. To talk of things being necessarily identical with themselves is, therefore, incorrect, since it suggests that the ascription of necessity depends only on the reference of a sign and not on the way in which the reference is made.

It may be objected that what I have been saying is true only of *de dicto* and not of *de re* modalities. My answer to this is that there are only *de dicto* modalities. The idea that things possess individual essences, independently of the way they are designated, is a metaphysical absurdity. Having once been discarded, it should never have been revived.

6 Self-Evidence

To say of a proposition that it is self-evident is to say not just that it is certainly true, but also that it does not stand in need of proof. One has only to understand the sentence which expresses it in order to be able to see that the proposition is true. Many philosophers have appealed to this notion of self-evidence, but there have been differences of opinion as to the range of propositions to which it can be applied. It has usually been taken to cover at least some of the true propositions of logic and mathematics, as well as propositions which are thought to be necessary in virtue of the non-logical concepts which they embody, such as the proposition that brothers are male siblings, or that whatever is red is coloured. Self-evidence has, however, also been ascribed to propositions which do not appear to fall into either of these categories, such as the proposition that every event has a cause, and some philosophers have claimed it for moral principles which they held to be true but saw no way of proving. An example might be that one ought not to take pleasure in another person's suffering.

The first point which emerges is that we cannot begin by taking the concept of self-evidence to coincide with that of being analytic. As we have just seen, self-evidence is claimed for propositions which at least do not appear to be incapable of being denied without contradiction; and conversely, many propositions which can plausibly be held to be analytic cannot with any plausibility be counted as self-evident. Logic and mathematics would be much easier subjects than they are if the conclusion of every theorem could be seen to be true, without the necessity of any proof.

A second point to note is that in saying of a proposition that it does not stand in need of proof, one should not be taken to imply that it is incapable of being proved. It might, indeed, be thought that when a proposition is capable of being proved, there would be nothing to gain, and perhaps something to lose, by holding it to be self-evident, but this would be to overlook the fact that deductive systems can have alternative bases. A proposition which appears as a premiss in one system may appear as the conclusion of a theorem in another. Consequently, if one is going to maintain that the premisses of a deductive system are self-evident, one may find oneself in the position of claiming self-evidence for propositions which one is also capable of proving.

A further distinction which we need to make at the outset is that between self-evident propositions, in the foregoing sense, and propositions for which certainty is claimed on the ground that in the circumstances in which they are advanced it makes no sense to doubt them. Propositions which are thought to be of this second sort are usually said to be incorrigible, the idea being that there is no possibility of a mistake which would call for their correction. In general, such incorrigibility has been claimed only for propositions which might be expressed by someone who was limiting himself to describing the nature of his present experience; propositions which would record his current thoughts or feelings or the quality of his sense-impressions; and it has been assumed that these propositions, being so limited in scope, would not carry any logical commitment to the occurrence of anything that was publicly observable: if they described the subject's current sense-impressions, their truth would not exclude the possibility of his being under some perceptual illusion. There are, however, philosophers, notably Wittgenstein,[1] who make substantially the same claim for propositions about the physical world which we unhesitatingly accept through the normal exercise of sense-perception or of memory, for those that record well-known historical facts, and even for propositions which express acknowledged scientific laws. They wish, in short, to confer a kind of immunity on all the propositions which it does not seriously occur to us to doubt; propositions which, for one reason or another, are so well established that to ask what is the evidence for them would seem out of place.

The difference between these so-called incorrigible propositions, in either extension of the term, and those that lay claim to self-evidence, in the sense that I first defined, is that self-evidence is supposed to be objective in a way that incorrigibility is not. The proposition that there is an expanse of green in the upper right-hand corner of my present visual field is arguably one of which the truth is known to me beyond any suspicion of doubt, but in that case it is

[1] See his book *On Certainty*.

only to me that it is known. Others who observe my situation may confidently infer that this is so, but they do not speak with the same authority. Again, anyone with normal vision would be able to see the tree which overhangs the terrace where I am seated, but he would need to be in my present neighbourhood: merely to understand the sentence that there exists a tree at such and such a place would not make it evident that what it expressed was true. Similarly, such pieces of common knowledge as that the battle of Hastings was fought in 1066 AD or that heating water causes it to boil rather than to freeze have had to be ascertained. There is nothing in these propositions, considered simply in themselves, that shows whether they are true or false. On the other hand, the truth of propositions which are said to be self-evident is supposed to be certifiable by anyone who understands the sentences which express them. It is sufficient to know what brothers are and what male siblings are in order to know for certain that brothers are male siblings. Anyone who has acquired the use of the mathematical concepts in question knows that $2 + 2 = 4$. Anyone who is morally enlightened knows that it is wrong to delight in another's pain.

The distinction is genuine, but there is a point at which it becomes tenuous. Does not one have to learn to reprehend cruelty, in very much the same way as one learns the facts of history or the rudiments of science? In so far as there is a difference is it not due to the fact that moral principles are themselves of a different order from propositions of these other sorts? Whatever this difference may be, it is surely not the case that one has only to understand what is meant by taking pleasure in another's pain and also to possess the concept of something's being wrong in order to see that they go together. The proof that it is not is that many people, who do possess these concepts, have indulged in cruelty without thinking it wrong. We can say that this shows them to be morally unenlightened, but what does this come to beyond the fact that their moral attitudes are different from ours? Or to take another of our examples, surely it is just not true that anyone who understands what an event is and what a cause is will come to see that every event must have a cause. If one's view of the world is thoroughly scientific and if the science of one's time is deterministic, one may indeed be led to regard this proposition as unquestionably true; but one may just as easily reject it if, as can well be the case, one or other of these conditions fails to hold.

But now it may be objected that I am picking out just those examples in which the pretension to self-evidence is most dubious. What upholds it is no more than that the principles in question are principles for which those who hold them can give no further reason: it is not positively sustained by any necessary relation between the concepts which are combined in them.

I think that this objection is well founded, but if we accept it the result will be that the candidature for self-evidence will be restricted to propositions for which the claim is also made that they are analytic. For if it is a necessary condition for a proposition to be self-evident that its truth can be determined simply through the consideration of the concepts which enter into it, then the only propositions which will qualify are those that are true in virtue of the meaning of the sentences which express them, and this is just the condition which is held to be sufficient for a proposition to be analytic. To say this is, indeed, to beg the question against those who hold that to apprehend the truth, say, of a proposition of elementary arithmetic, one has not only to command the relevant concepts but also to depend on *a priori* intuition. Since, however, the power to exercise this intuition is supposed to accrue to anyone who does command the concepts, the question is one that we can afford to beg in the present context. For even if it turned out that the claims to analyticity had been too generously accorded, the restrictions on the claims to self-evidence would remain the same.

The difficulty lies rather in the other direction. Since it is admitted that not all necessary propositions, whether or not we reckon them all as analytic, are self-evident, where is the line to be drawn? How is it decided whether such propositions stand in need of proof? Is it simply a question of the terms on which we are willing to accept them? In some cases we should demand that proof be given, in others their truth would seem so obvious that to insist upon a proof would seem superfluous or even misguided. But clearly this is not a distinction about which there is likely to be any very general agreement. Not only do people differ in their perspicacity, but they differ in their standards of rigour. Most of us are content to take the truth of such a proposition as that $2 + 2 = 4$ on trust. A logician who is engaged in the enterprise of reducing mathematics to logic may take volumes to prove it. This may result even in his deriving propositions which seem to us self-evident from ones that do not. The single proposition to which Nicod reduced the primitive propositions of Russell's and Whitehead's *Principia Mathematica* is far too complicated for its truth to be obvious at a glance. Neither do we have to take it on trust. We can test it by the truth-tables and find that it comes out as a tautology.

The fact that there are differences of opinion as to what we are entitled to accept without proof does not itself entail that nothing qualifies for such acceptance. But the argument may be pressed further. The question may be raised whether someone's being certain that such and such is so is ever a sufficient reason for concluding that it is so. If we set aside propositions like '*A* exists' or '*A* is animated' which have to be true if it is to be true that *A* believes anything at all, does '*p*' ever follow logically from '*A* believes that *p*'? Except in the trivial sense in which a necessary proposition follows from any proposition whatsoever, it is not at all certain that it ever does. The doubtful cases are those of allegedly incorrigible propositions, in the narrower extension of the term. There is some plausibility in the idea of its not being logically possible, so long as merely linguistic errors are excluded, for anyone falsely to believe that he is in pain, or falsely to believe that there is an expanse of green in his present visual field, though even here I am inclined to think that one can devise counterexamples. There is no question but that one can misidentify the character of one's feelings or the qualities of one's sense-impressions, and the problem is only that of deciding when, if ever, such a mistake is to count as being factual and when as being merely verbal. Very often, I think, the distinction will be fairly arbitrary. However this may be, these are in any case not among the propositions which are thought to be generally self-evident. Even if, in appropriate conditions, they have their own way of being certain, they are not necessarily true. And when it comes to propositions which are taken to be necessary, then the answer to the question whether their truth is ever logically guaranteed by their being believed is surely that it never is. Whatever the example chosen, the fact that someone is convinced that some proposition of this sort is true will always be consistent with its not being true. In such a case, the only way in which the proposition that *A* is mistaken in believing that *p* can turn out to be contradictory is that if '*p*' is indeed necessarily true, then one will oneself be expressing a necessary falsehood in implicitly denying it.

This is not to say that people's convictions count for nothing. If *A* is known to be a competent mathematician, his acceptance of some proposition which he claims to have been proved will be a good reason for our believing it to be true, even though we are not ourselves capable of following the proof. If he declares some step in the argument to be obvious, we shall allow that he is justified in making it, even though it is by no means obvious to us. The admission that he is not infallible, that there is indeed no point at which it is not logically possible that he should be mistaken, does not divest him of all authority. But the source of his authority is not the strength of his convictions but rather the fact that they have consistently or at any rate frequently turned out to be right. We take his word because we know that on previous occasions when he has given it his claims have been tested and certified.

But now the argument turns the other way. For how, we may ask, have his claims been certified? By the consensus of opinion among other mathematicians who have satisfied themselves that his proofs were in order; that their premisses were true and that the conclusions followed from them. No doubt the premisses would be propositions which had already been established, but for them to be established the same conditions would have to have been fulfilled. Again it is not necessary that the first links in the chain should simply be taken on trust. There may be procedures by which they can be checked. But then it has to be assumed that these requirements really are met, when they appear to be. It has also to be assumed that one step in the proof does really follow from another. Here too there may be methods of checking, but in the end there will be nothing for it but just to be able to see that things come out right. And what is this, it may be asked, but a final appeal to self-evidence?

Once more this is not to deny that mistakes are always possible. The point is rather that the process of proof must somewhere come to an end. If every step in a deductive argument had to be licensed by a special premiss, then, as Lewis Carroll showed in his Achilles paradox,[2] no conclusion could ever be drawn. The tortoise, in his fable, accepts '*p*' and 'if *p* then *q*' but requires to be shown that this is sufficient for the conclusion that *q*. He argues that there is a need of the extra premiss: 'If (if *p*, and if *p* then *q*), then *q*'. But then when Achilles adds this premiss to the others, the tortoise is still not satisfied. He requires the further premiss: 'If [if *p*, and if *p* then *q*,

---

[2] See his 'What the Tortoise said to Achilles', *Mind* IV (N.S., 1895), pp. 278–80.

and if (if *p*, and if *p* then *q*), then *q*], then *q*' and so *ad infinitum.* The moral is that a rule of inference is something to be followed. If it is made explicit, and posited as a premiss, it loses its function. There will then be need for another rule. One wants to say that someone who accepts '*p*' and accepts 'If *p* then *q*' is thereby committed to accepting '*q*'. His recognition of this commitment is a mark of his understanding of the expression 'If . . . then'. He has, indeed, to see that he is committed, but this need come to no more than his being able to apply the rule. It can be explained to him, but he has to grasp it.

Are we then able to say that it is self-evident that if (if *p*, and if *p* then *q*), then *q*? What point should we be making? As a proposition, it can be proved, either by deduction from a set of logical axioms, such as the axioms of *Principia Mathematica*, or by consulting the truth-tables and finding that it comes out true under every assignment of truth-values to '*p*' and '*q*'. No doubt there are many people who can see at a glance that it is true, but that is of little interest, unless we are concerned with testing their intelligence. On the other hand, if it is taken as a rule, then the point is that it is straightforwardly applied. There could, indeed, be a rule which directed how it was to be applied; we might, for example, be instructed to detach the consequent if and only if the antecedent had been found to satisfy certain criteria of proof, and there could even be a directive for interpreting this rule; but the supply of directives has to give out somewhere. At some point, we have just to understand what we are expected to do, and act accordingly.

The analogy of a game may be helpful here. Suppose that I am playing a beginner at chess, and that I say 'Checkmate' and he says 'Prove it', I point out that the position of his king in relation to my bishop entails that it is in check, that, according to the rules and in view of the positions of the other pieces, there are just so many squares to which his king can move, that if it moves to this square it will be in check from the other bishop, if it moves to that square it will be in check from the knight, and so on until I have covered all the possibilities. His recognition that this is so goes together with his understanding how to play the game. It is of course logically possible that there is something which we have both overlooked, that there is, for example, a piece which he can interpose. It is logically possible that I have misremembered the rules of chess. It is logically possible that our vision is at fault, so that we are both mistaken in thinking that the king and the bishop are aligned, with no other piece in between them. There is, however, not very much that we can do about these possibilities, beyond making the formal admission that they do exist. We can look up the rules, in which case we shall be assuming that they are correctly stated and that we are reading them correctly. Having made these assumptions, we are then just left to note how the rules apply to this particular case. If we think it necessary to check our eyesight, we can have it tested by an oculist, or we can call in a third person to inspect the board. But then we have to understand what these persons tell us. There is always the possibility of error, and there are always further tests that we can resort to. If I am doing a sum in arithmetic I can go over it again and again, I can call on any number of people to check it for me; I can have recourse to a computer, and them employ a second computer to check on the first. In the end, however, it must always come down to my just being satisfied that I have got it right; and, unless I am very neurotic, this will happen quite early. If I am adding up a column of figures, it will probably be enough for me that I add it upwards and downwards and get the same result. The most timid householder does not usually make more than one inspection to make sure that he has safely locked the door.

The point is that a test serves no purpose unless we are disposed to accept what it appears to show. If its result is surprising, we may reasonably require that it be corroborated, but again this will be futile if the corroboration, when it comes, is not to be taken at its face value. As I said earlier, the process of proof must come to an end somewhere; not indeed to an absolute end, since any question can be reopened, but to the point where we are satisfied, where we see no use in carrying it any further. And just for this reason there are very many cases in which the need for proof does not arise. These are the cases in which we are satisfied straight away, because the results of our calculations, or the interpretations that we put on what is presented to our senses, fit in with our existing stock of beliefs. We take it for granted that the outcome of any further experiments would be favourable, at least so long as they themselves were not suspect. Indeed, the only point of making them would be to add to the volume of evidence, since the conclusions at which we have arrived already have as strong a claim to credence as those that would result from any further test.

The attraction which philosophers have found in strictly incorrigible propositions has been that they seemed to provide an absolutely secure basis for knowledge. If their truth really did follow from their being believed, at least by the person to whose current experience they referred, there was not even the possibility of their being upset by any other evidence. Admittedly, their immunity lasted only so long as the fleeting experience which they monitored, but at least they brought the whole structure of our beliefs repeatedly into firm contact with the earth. They prevented it being left to hang in the air with its array of propositions defending only one another.

There is no doubt that this function needs to be performed, but it is dubious whether incorrigible propositions are needed to perform it. Is there really any profit in a security which so quickly vanishes? What we must have are rules of meaning which correlate the signs that we use with observable states of affairs. Even in the employment of a purely formal language, we need to be able to tell that such and such a mark or sound is an instance of such and such a numeral, or whatever it may be. It does not, however, seem to be necessary that our rules of meaning should be such as to apply without any possibility of error, or even that they should rest upon any such foundation. As I have suggested elsewhere,[3] we might very well manage with rules which licensed us to accept a sentence when there was no more than a high probability that the state of affairs with which it was correlated did in fact obtain. Indeed, it is with rules of this sort that we actually do manage. A child learns to use the names of physical objects under conditions where it is always at least logically possible that he is undergoing an illusion, so that the object in question is not really there. The occasions when this actually happens are, however, so infrequent, and the mistakes to which they give rise so easily corrected, that the risk he is made to run is negligible. We could begin by teaching him to name his sense-impressions, but the gain in security would be outweighed by the lack of interest in what he would be learning to communicate. In the normal way our sense-impressions are of importance to us only as the springboard from which to jump to conclusions about what is physically present, and it is to the expression of these conclusions that our rules of meaning are adapted. If one is philosophically concerned with the analysis of perception, there may, indeed, be an

---

[3] See my article on 'Basic Propositions'. Reprinted in my *Philosophical Essays*.

advantage in introducing ways of speaking which make these inferences explicit, but no such terminology is required to give our language a sufficient anchorage in empirical fact.

In any event, no rules of meaning which operate at the level of observation can be expected to legislate with certainty for every possible case. There is likely always to be an area of imprecision within which it is not clear either that the term in question applies or that it does not. This is conspicuously so in the case of colours, where the fact that shades of colour spread over a continuous range entails that we repeatedly come upon borderline stretches where it is uncertain where one shade ends and another begins. This example may also serve to show how dangerous it can be to trust one's intuition. Thus, it might appear self-evident that if one object, A, displays some specific shade of red, and another object, B, is indistinguishable in colour from A, it also displays that shade. What else do we mean by their being indistinguishable? And then by the same principle, if B displays that shade and a third object, C, is indistinguishable in colour from B, C too will display it. But then, if the different shades of red are qualitatively continuous, it will follow that there are no different shades. For what is implied by their forming a continuum is that it is always possible to find a set of objects A, B, C, all falling withing their extension, such that A is indistinguishable in colour from B, and B from C, but that A is distinguishable from C. In short, it is an empirical fact that the relation of being indistinguishable in colour is not transitive. It is for this reason that we are able to travel along a continuous line from one shade of colour to another. But now if we make what seems the obvious assumption that two objects which are indistinguishable in colour display the same shade, we render this relation transitive, and thereby abolish all the shades but one. Worse still, if, as appears to be the case, the colours in the spectrum form a continuous sequence, we reach the absurd conclusion that everything is of exactly the same colour. To avoid it we have to allow, contrary to our intuition, that it is not a sufficient condition for B to display the same shade of colour as A that the two should be indistinguishable in colour. It is necessary also that there be no object from which one of them is distinguishable in colour and the other not.

This is a very strong condition, so strong indeed that there seems to be no way of making completely sure that any two objects satisfy it. We cannot examine all the objects that there are, and so long as even one remains unexamined, there is always the possibility that it would separate our pair. But surely we do continually judge with confidence what colour things look to us to be, and consequently whether or not the same colour term applies to them. Surely I can properly claim to know that the leaves on this branch above me are all now looking green. The answer is that I can apply terms like 'green' with confidence because of their comparative lack of precision. They apply to a range of objects which need not be indistinguishable in colour but are required to match one another roughly within limits that are not clear-cut. The sufficient condition for any two objects to satisfy such a term is again that they match just the same objects in the appropriate way. But in that case, since the matching need be only rough, we can be sure that this condition is fulfilled by objects, like these leaves, which come as it were in the middle of the range. There will, indeed, be objects with regard to which it is not clear whether they come within this range or another, but their existence does not threaten to separate the objects in the centre. To the extent that it is uncertain whether any such penumbral object matches any one of these leaves to a sufficient degree, it will be equally uncertain whether it matches the others. What follows is that the colour of the penumbral objects, for example, the objects which occupy the borderline between green and blue, cannot be certainly determined, but that is a tolerable consequence.

It does not matter to us that such concepts are vague because the instances which fall upon their outskirts are relatively few, and they can anyhow be adequately characterized as belonging to the border zone of two neighbouring ranges. It is only if we wish to determine shades with such precision that any two objects which are discriminable in colour are held to display different shades, that all attributions become uncertain. And the same applies to any other domain, such as that of sound, where the relation of being indistinguishable in such and such a respect is discovered not to be transitive. It is an empirical fact that there are these qualitative continuities, so that the vagueness in which we take refuge is not a logical necessity. There seems, however, to be no practical prospect of eliminating it.

If, as is normally the case, our rules of meaning relate to physical objects, their application will be rendered uncertain not only by vagueness but also by the fact, which we have already noted, that the existence of the things to which our signs refer will not be logically guaranteed by our having the experiences which justify their use. To continue with our example, it would, indeed, be absurd for me to entertain any serious doubt whether these really are green leaves. I have no reason to suppose that my senses are not functioning normally; my memory assures me that this tree has been here for years. I calculate that I must have seen it thousands of times. In summer its leaves are always green. Nevertheless, in making this perceptual judgement, I am going beyond the content of my present sense-experience. I am putting an interpretation upon my visual data which could conceivably be wrong. It is logically possible that I am undergoing an illusion. It is logically possible that my memory is playing me false. And this will remain the case, whatever further tests I carry out. The possibility that future experiences will lead me to revise my judgement can never be logically excluded.

But now we come back to the point that there is nothing to be done about these possibilities beyond just noting that they exist. They simply mark the fact that all our ordinary judgements draw drafts upon the future, and any draft upon the future can be dishonoured. So long, however, as we have no positive reason to believe that they will be dishonoured, the scepticism to which we are committed is purely formal. It becomes of interest only when it is brought to bear not on particular judgements, which are acknowledged to be fallible, but on the whole system of concepts which these judgements embody. But then we need arguments to show that these concepts are defective, and some grounds for thinking that a different system would serve us better.

Whatever system we adopt, there will be a great deal that we take for granted. Not only our common understanding of the meanings of the words we use, but also our ability to follow rules of inference; not only methodological principles and criteria of evidence, but a mass of historical and scientific information. We have moral and aesthetic principles for which it is arguable that no justification can be provided outside themselves. We have seen that various distinctions can be made with regard to the question how much of all this is to be regarded as self-evident, but this turns out also not to be a question of primary interest. The important points are that we learn in the end just to be able to see what a rule demands of us, and that any process of proof must come to a halt somewhere. It is, however, also true that any question can be reopened and that the whole of our system, both the beliefs which enter into it and the processes by which they are formed, is liable to change. We cannot change it all at once, because we should then have no standpoint from which to change it, but no part of it is sacrosanct, not even its necessary propositions, including its laws of logic, since although they are dictated to us by the terms which figure in them, we might find it convenient to use different terms. We are limited only by a principle of consistency, which ensures that whatever move may be open to us, when we have made a given move, we have made that move and not a different one. For this is the minimal condition of our having any system at all.

To say that a proposition is self-evident is never an argument. At best it is an invitation to one's audience to look at things again, in cases where if they are unable to see them as we do, we have no further argument to offer.

7 *Wittgenstein on Certainty*

Wittgenstein's book *On Certainty*, which was first published in 1969, eighteen years after his death, is a collection of notes which he composed during the last eighteen months of his life. As his editors explain in their preface, these notes, which were written at four different periods, are all in the form of a first draft. They are more repetitive than they no doubt would have been if Wittgenstein had been able to revise them. Even so, they are characteristically succinct and penetrating, and the argument which they develop is easier to follow than that of the general run of Wittgenstein's later work.

The peg on which the argument is hung is that of G. E. Moore's defence of common sense. Moore had attempted to safeguard what he called the common-sense view of the world against the arguments of philosophers who doubted or denied it simply by claiming that he knew it to be true. For instance, he took it to be part of this common-sense view 'that there are in the Universe enormous numbers of material objects',[1] which exist in space and time, and he construed this proposition in such a way that it followed from a set of particular propositions, such as that he had a body which had existed for some time and during that time had been 'in contact with or not far from the surface of the earth', that there had at the same time existed many other things, 'also having shape and size in three dimensions', from which his body had been at various distances, that these things included other human bodies, and that many things of these different kinds, including the earth itself, had existed for many years before he was born.[2] These were all propositions which he claimed to know for certain to be true, and he also claimed that the truth of propositions corresponding to these was known for certain to many other people. In the same way, he attempted on one occasion to prove the existence of external objects simply by holding

[1] G. E. Moore, *Some Main Problems of Philosophy*, p. 2.
[2] G. E. Moore, 'A Defence of Common Sense', *Philosophical Papers*, pp. 32–5.

up his two hands, and saying that the propositions 'Here is one hand' and 'Here is another' were known by him to be true. And a little later, by recalling that he had held up his hands some time before, he proved that external objects had also existed in the past.[3]

The point of this procedure is that if Moore really did know what he claimed to know, it would follow that any philosopher who denied the truth of any such propositions, or even held it to be doubtful whether any of them were true, must be wrong. For what is known to be true cannot fail to be so, whatever arguments may be mustered on the other side. It might then appear that the question to be answered was whether Moore's claims were justified.

In a way, Wittgenstein does address himself to this question, but not straightforwardly. He is concerned rather to show that it does not seriously arise. He does not deny the truth, or even the certainty, of propositions of the sorts that Moore took for his examples. On the contrary, he maintains that to express any doubt of their truth, in normal circumstances, would be nonsensical. At the same time, he argues that if it were significant to doubt them, it would not be sufficient to allay the doubt for anyone just to say that he knew them to be true. Not only that, but Moore was, in his view, actually at fault in saying this. The reason why he held him to be at fault was not that the propositions themselves were any less certain than Moore took them to be, but that to say, in the circumstances in which Moore did say them, such things as 'I know that this is a hand' or 'I know that the earth has existed for many years past' was a misuse of the expression 'I know'.

Let us begin with the point that merely to say that one knows a proposition to be true is not an acceptable method of proving it. If one is asked for a proof of some proposition which one believes, something more is required than the bare statement that one is convinced of its truth. But what difference is there between saying that one is certain that something is so and saying that one knows that it is so? There is no important difference, says Wittgenstein, 'except where "I know" is meant to mean: I *can't* be wrong'.[4] But then this claim has to be justified. As Wittgenstein puts it, 'It needs to be *shown* that no mistake was possible.'[5] Some objective reason has to be given for concluding that I must be right.

Philosophers get the idea that if they know something they cannot

---

[3] G. E. Moore, 'Proof of an External World', *Philosophical Papers*, pp. 146–8.
[4] *On Certainty*, 8.   [5] *OC*, 15.

be mistaken about it, because the use of the word 'know' carries the implication that what is known is true. If some proposition which I thought I knew turns out not to be true, it will follow logically that I did not know it. This is not, however, to say that my state of mind was other than what I took it to be, as if I had confused the mental attitude of knowledge with that of mere belief. My feeling of certainty might be exactly the same, whether I knew the proposition to be true or whether I only thought I knew it. It might be said that the feeling was justified in the one case and not in the other, but the difference then would lie not in the quality of the feeling but in the status of the proposition in question and the grounds that there might be for accepting it.

It follows that if one is seeking to be assured of the truth of some proposition, the fact of someone's saying that he knows it to be true will not meet the purpose unless one has some good reason for believing what he says. Even if his honesty is not in doubt, we have to be satisfied that he is in a position to have acquired this piece of knowledge, and we have also to be satisfied that the proposition which he claims to know is one for which there are sufficient grounds. If we are not satisfied on either of these counts, we shall be prompted to ask him how he knows, or what makes him think he knows, whatever it may be. In the more common case, in which we are less concerned with his standing as an informant than with the value of the information that he professes to be giving us, we shall in effect be asking him for evidence that what he says he knows is really so.

There are two conditions that have to be fulfilled, if this demand is to be met. The evidence which he supplies must give adequate support to the proposition in question; and it must itself consist of one or more propositions which we have a sufficient ground for taking to be true. But then, if this means that these propositions have to be supported in their turn by further propositions for which we have to furnish sufficient grounds, we are in danger of embarking on an infinite regress. To put a stop to the regress, we must at some point come to propositions which are acceptable in their own right. Such propositions will owe their security, not to the support of other propositions, but to their own content or to the conditions under which they are expressed.

Wittgenstein does not deny that this is so. Indeed, he treats Moore's examples as propositions of this sort. What he does deny is that we can legitimately speak of such propositions as being known to be true. Reviewing Moore's procedure, he remarks, quite correctly, that the point of Moore's examples is not that they furnish information which others might not have. They are, and are intended to be, typical of propositions which, in the appropriate circumstances, we all accept without question. And this suggests to him that in saying, in the way that Moore does, 'I *know*, I am not just surmising, that here is my hand' one is expressing not an ordinary empirical proposition but 'a proposition of grammar'. To prove in this way that there are physical objects is like proving that there are colours by saying 'I know, I am not just surmising, that I am seeing red.'[6] The implication is, I suppose, that these propositions embody rules of meaning. To deny, in these circumstances, that that was a hand or that I was seeing red would be to show oneself ignorant of what the words 'hand' and 'red' were used to mean.

But then, Wittgenstein argues, 'If "I know etc." is conceived as a grammatical proposition . . . it properly means "There is no such thing as a doubt in this case" or "The expression 'I do not know' makes no sense in this case." And of course it follows from this that "I *know*" makes no sense either.'[7]

Is this so? Let us set aside for the moment the more interesting question whether the proposition 'Here is a hand' has, in these circumstances, the same title to certainty as the proposition 'I am seeing red', and consider only the proposition that I am seeing red, where this is taken to imply no more than that the colour red is exemplified in my present visual field. If this proposition is true, does it make no sense to say that I do not know that it is true? And if it were senseless for me to say that I did not know it to be true, would it automatically follow that it was also senseless for me to say that I did know this?

I am not convinced that Wittgenstein gives the right answer to either of these questions. It is surely possible for someone to be seeing a colour which he fails to identify correctly, and in that case the statement that he did not know what colour he was seeing, so far from being senseless, would be true. But would this, in the present case, prove anything more than that he had not learned how to use the English word 'red'? On the assumption that he does understand what this word means, would it not be senseless for him to say that

[6] *OC*, 57.   [7] *OC*, 58.

he did not know whether he was seeing red or not? Even this seems
to me doubtful. It is true that if someone were always at a loss to say
whether or not a given colour-term applied to what he saw, we
should infer that he had not learned the meaning of the term, but
this does not oblige us to conclude that he is ignorant of its meaning,
if there are any occasions on which he hesitates. For instance, I think
that I know perfectly well what the words 'blue' and 'green' mean;
yet there are times when I am not sure which of them to use. There
are also times when, having used one of them, I am asked to look
again and then decide that I ought to have used the other.

It could still be argued that these were cases of verbal and not
factual uncertainty. I do not find this convincing, but I do not want
to make an issue of it. For let it be granted, for the sake of argument,
that the truth of a man's descriptions of the colours which he sees is
always a test of his understanding what the colour-words in question
mean. The consequence of this will be that the proposition that he
both understands what the word 'red' means and does not know
whether what he sees is red becomes self-contradictory. It can be
characterized as senseless only if one takes what seems the
unwarranted step of denying any sense to contradictions. But then it
certainly will not follow that the proposition that he knows that what
he sees is red is also senseless. On the contrary, the premises which
exclude its negation must entail that it is true.

The same conclusion can be reached in another way. For someone
to know that a proposition is true, it is sufficient that it be true, that
he be confident of its truth, and that he have the right sort of
grounds for this confidence. In the present instance, there is no
doubt that the first two conditions are satisfied. All that can be in
question is the third. But what better ground can he have for
believing that he sees such-and-such a colour than the actual
appearance of what he takes to be that colour in his present visual
field? It is true that he may not be able to say how he knows that he
is seeing this colour, if this is taken as requiring him to adduce some
other proposition which supports his claim. He may have no other
course than to repeat that this is what he sees. But if in order to
know the truth of any proposition, we had always to know the truth
of some other proposition which supported it, then, as I have
already remarked, we should be committed to an infinite regress. At
some stage our claims to knowledge must be founded directly on
experience. This does not require us to hold that our accounts of

what we are experiencing can never be mistaken. Even if I am the final authority with regard to my own sensations, I can sometimes find cause to revise my judgements of their qualities. The point at issue is that these are judgements for which one is not required to give any further reasons, beyond the actual occurrence of the data which they monitor. This is not, however, a ground for saying that we cannot know them to be true. The anomaly would rather lie in representing our knowledge as sustained by propositions which could not themselves significantly be said to be known.

What may have led Wittgenstein astray here is the fact that statements like 'I know that this looks red to me' or even 'I know that this is a hand' would only exceptionally serve any purpose. There are no common occasions for their use. In the ordinary way, the point of saying 'I know that so and so' is either to show that one has acquired some information which one may have been thought not to possess, or else to insist on the truth of some proposition, which has been or might be seriously challenged. In either case saying 'I know' gives an assurance which is assumed to be needed. But when the proposition in question is that I am seeing some familiar colour, or that these are my hands, there is normally no need for any such assurance. It is taken for granted that I can recognize ordinary colours: the proposition that these are my hands is not, in this context, one that anybody is seriously inclined to doubt. If someone were learning English and were engaged in mastering the use of English colour-words, there would be some point in his saying that he knew that what he saw was red. A man who had suffered a brain lesion which rendered him incapable of recognizing ordinary objects might say to his doctor that he knew at least that these were his hands, as a way of marking the progress of his recovery. But these are exceptional circumstances. In the cases which Wittgenstein envisages, the objection to saying 'I know that . . .' is that it suggests that the circumstances are exceptional, when they are not.

From this we can conclude not only that the use of the expression 'I know that' may serve no purpose, but that it may be actually misleading. It does not, however, follow that its use in such cases is senseless, or even that it is not used to state what is true. This may be illustrated by another example. Although people most commonly believe what they assert, the conventional effect of prefacing an assertion with the words 'I believe that' is to weaken its force. It suggests that one is not entirely sure of what follows. If I say, for instance, 'I believe that Smith has been elected' I commit myself less than if I had said outright: 'Smith has been elected'. Nevertheless, it certainly does not follow that when I do assert something outright, I do not believe it. In exactly the same way, the fact that it may be pointless or even misleading for me to say such things as 'I know that this looks red to me' or 'I know that these are my hands' in no way entails that what I am saying is not true.

If statements of these sorts are very often true, does it follow that what one knows is certain? The difficulty with this question is to understand what certainty means. There is, as Wittgenstein said, a sense of the word 'certain' in which to ask whether a proposition is certain is just a way of asking whether it is known to be true, and in that sense, evidently, every proposition which is known to be true is certain. In Wittgenstein's special sense, which is perhaps only philosophical, a proposition, as we have seen, can be said to be certain only if it is inconceivable that one should be mistaken in thinking it true, and in that sense it is doubtful if the word has any application, at any rate to empirical propositions. It is, indeed, very unlikely that a man will be mistaken in his description of the way things look and feel to him, but I think, as I have said, that it has to be admitted as a possibility. Another mainly philosophical sense is that in which a proposition is said to be certain only if it is necessarily true. This is a condition which empirical propositions do not satisfy, though we shall see later on that where Wittgenstein attributes certainty to empirical propositions, he assimilates them to propositions of logic.

When philosophers talk about certainty, they also often treat it as a matter of degree. Thus, a philosopher who does not deny the truth of such a proposition as that there are trees in his garden, or even deny that there is a perfectly proper sense in which he can be said to know that it is true, may still wish to say that it is less certain than some proposition which records his current visual or tactual sensations. His reason for this will be just that by claiming more it runs the greater risk of being false. My descriptions of the colours which are exemplified in my present visual field may still be true even though I am dreaming or hallucinated. They may still be true even though the interpretations which I put upon my visual data are not corroborated by the tactual data which they would lead me to expect, or by the reports which I receive from other observers. This does not apply, however, to such a proposition as that there are trees in my garden. It is true that I accept it, on the basis of what I think I see, or remember, without looking for any further evidence. I take it for granted that the necessary corroboration would be forthcoming. Even so my present experience does not guarantee that it would be forthcoming, and if it were discovered not to be I should have reason to conclude that I had been mistaken. It is on this ground that philosophers like Russell have concluded that no proposition which implied the existence of a physical object was altogether certain. What they meant was that no such proposition ever logically followed from any set of propositions which merely recorded the content of one's current sense-experiences.

The logical point is sound, but it might have been better to make it more straightforwardly. The trouble is that one tends to forget that the word 'uncertain' is being used here in a technical sense, in which to say that all propositions which imply the existence of physical objects are uncertain is to say no more than that they do not follow from some limited set of propositions which refer only to sense-qualia. One tends to make it carry the further implication that these propositions about physical objects cannot be known to be true, that they are all of them seriously open to doubt. And indeed it would seem that Russell himself did think this to be so, at least during the periods when he held that physical objects were external causes of our percepts. Though he thought that the character of our percepts gave us some good reason to believe in these external causes, he also thought it to be a genuine possibility that they did not exist.

Rather than accept this conclusion, we should most of us nowadays either try to argue that it did not follow from the causal theory of perception, or else, if we believed that it did follow, regard this as a decisive argument against the theory. But are we right? What is there about our belief in the physical world that makes it sacrosanct?

Wittgenstein's answer to this is that it is not an ordinary factual belief, but rather part of the frame of reference within which the truth or falsehood of our factual beliefs is assessed. As he puts it, 'All testing, all confirmation and disconfirmation of a hypothesis takes place already within a system. And this system is not a more or less arbitrary and doubtful point of departure for all our arguments: no, it belongs to the essence of what we call an argument. The system is not so much the point of departure, as the element in which arguments have their life.'[8] The system is not, indeed, entirely sacrosanct, since it is susceptible of change, but its propositions can be said to be immune from doubt, in the sense that, so long as they hold their place in the system, it does not occur to us to doubt them. 'What prevents me', asks Wittgenstein, 'from supposing that this table either vanishes or alters its shape and colour when no one is observing it, and then, when someone looks at it again, changes back to its old condition? – "But who is going to suppose such a thing?" – one would feel like saying.'[9] And then he continues: 'Here we see that the idea of "agreement with reality" does not have any clear application.'[10] I take it that what he means by this is that it is only in the light of certain assumptions that the notion of agreement with reality comes into play. The assumptions themselves neither agree nor disagree with reality. They determine the nature of the reality with which agreement is sought.

How far do these assumptions extend? This is not an easy question to answer because the system is not clearly defined. Wittgenstein speaks of it as an inherited world-picture and of its propositions as being 'part of a kind of mythology'.[11] 'It might be imagined', he says, 'that some propositions, of the form of empirical propositions, were hardened and functioned as channels for such empirical propositions as were not hardened but fluid; and that this relation altered with time, in that fluid propositions hardened and hard ones became fluid. The mythology may change back into a state of flux, the river-bed of thoughts may shift. But I distinguish between the movement of the waters on the river-bed and the shift of the bed itself; though there is not a sharp division of the one from the other. But if someone were to say "So logic too is an empirical science" he would be wrong. Yet this is right: the same proposition may get treated at one time as something to test by experience, at another as a rule of testing.'[12]

The suggestion is that there is no clear-cut boundary either between the *a priori* propositions of logic and mathematics and some propositions that would ordinarily be counted as empirical, or between these propositions and those of which the empirical character is not in doubt. If it is the mark of a necessary proposition that it is not exposed to empirical refutation, then the

[8] *OC*, 105.   [9] *OC*, 214.   [10] *OC*, 215.
[11] *OC*, 95.   [12] *OC*, 96–8.

propositions of logic and mathematics are indeed necessary, but the fact that it is possible to make mistakes in mathematics and logic has the consequence that we cannot always be sure of the conclusions to which they seem to lead us. All the same, there is nothing else for us to rely on than our impression that we are following the rules. When we have checked and rechecked a simple calculation, the suggestion that we may still be in error is not taken seriously. If someone were seriously to regard all our calculations as uncertain, we might think he was mad, or perhaps only that he was very different from ourselves. 'We rely on calculations, he doesn't; we are sure, he isn't'.[13] In the same way, if we come upon a fundamentalist who genuinely believes that the world came into existence in the year 4004 BC, with delusive appearances of much greater antiquity, we have no way of proving that he is wrong. Any evidence which we take as showing that the world really has existed for many millions of years can be taken by him as showing that the world presents the appearance of having existed for many millions of years before it really did exist. In the end, if we don't consider him mad, we have again to fall back on saying that he is simply different from us; he does not accept our canons of evidence.

It is the same with the sceptic, who argues that since our memories sometimes deceive us, they may do so always. As Russell once said: 'There is no logical impossibility in the hypothesis that the world sprang into being five minutes ago, exactly as it then was, with a population that "remembered" a wholly unreal past.'[14] This is a proposition which no sane man believes, but it cannot be disproved. We can check one memory-belief against another, but there is no way, free from circularity, of justifying memory in general, any more than there is a non-circular way of justifying induction. In the case of induction, indeed, it is not so much a matter of our adopting a set of general assumptions, as of acquiring certain habits of inference. 'Do we not', says Wittgenstein, 'simply follow the principle that what has always happened will happen again (or something like it)? What does it mean to follow this principle? Do we really introduce it into our reasoning? Or is it merely the *natural law* which our inferring apparently follows? This latter it may be. It is not an item in our considerations.'[15]

[13] *OC*, 217.   [14] *The Analysis of Mind*, p. 151   [15] *OC*, 135.

To say that this inductive principle is not introduced into our reasoning is not to say that our reasoning does not presuppose it. The fact is, however, that the principle that what has always happened will happen again is too general and, indeed, too vague to sustain the inferences that we actually make. Not only is not every observed uniformity thought to be projectible, but by a suitable choice of predicates we can create as much uniformity as we please. We rely, therefore, not on a general assumption about the uniformity of nature, but on a set of hypotheses about the special ways in which it repeats itself. Such hypotheses are indeed already incorporated in our idea of 'what has always happened'. The predicates which we use to describe events themselves embody assumptions to the effect that such properties invariably go together.

In this matter, there is no clear distinction between the hypotheses which enter into the common-sense view of the world and those that we obtain from science. There is at most a difference of degree. Thus, one of Wittgenstein's examples of a proposition which might be said to be certain is the proposition that water boils at about 100 °C. It would, as he says, be accepted unconditionally in a court of law.[16] Even so, the place which such a proposition occupies in our scheme of thought is not entirely secure. If it did come to grief we should not feel that the order of nature had been overturned. Indeed, Wittgenstein himself goes some way towards acknowledging this. 'If', he says, 'I now say "I know that the water in the kettle on the gas-flame will not freeze but boil", I seem to be as justified in this "I know" as I am in *any*. "If I know anything I know *this*." – Or do I know with still *greater* certainty that the person opposite me is my old friend so-and-so? And how does that compare with the proposition that I am seeing with two *eyes* and shall see them if I look in the glass? – I don't know confidently what I am to answer here. – But still there is a difference between the cases. If the water over the gas freezes, of course I shall be as astonished as can be, but I shall assume some factor I don't know of, and perhaps leave the matter to physicists to judge. But what could make me doubt whether this person here is N. N., whom I have known for years? Here a doubt would seem to drag everything with it and plunge it into chaos.'[17]

[16] OC, 604.　　　　　[17] OC, 613.

It would, indeed, be astonishing if the water froze, but science itself prepares us for surprises. Events which were thought to be impossible are found to occur, arouse a passing wonderment, and are then accepted as a matter of course. How quickly we have assimilated the idea of the moon's being accessible to us! The later journeys of the American astronauts barely make the headlines. Yet this was one of the things that Wittgenstein, writing only a little more than twenty years ago, felt confident in excluding. 'If', he said, 'we are thinking within our system, then it is certain that no one has ever been on the moon. Not merely is nothing of the sort ever seriously reported to us by reasonable people, but our whole system of physics forbids us to believe it. For this demands answers to the questions "How did he overcome the force of gravity?" "How could he live without an atmosphere?" and a thousand others which could not be answered. But suppose that instead of all these answers we met the reply: "We don't know *how* man gets to the moon, but those who get there know at once that they are there; and even you can't explain everything." We should feel ourselves intellectually very distant from someone who said this.'[18]

The example is unfortunate, but perhaps it needs only to be changed a little. Should we not feel ourselves intellectually very distant from someone who said the same thing about Mars? It very much depends on who 'we' are. In 1938, before there was any serious thought of man's going to the moon, a realistic broadcast of Wells's *The Shape of Things to Come* persuaded millions of Americans that men from Mars had invaded the United States. Thousands of Catholics, including at least one Pope, have believed in the 'miracle of Fatima', according to which sometime earlier in this century the sun left the sky, advanced towards the earth, opened to disclose the Virgin Mary, and then returned to its position, all without doing any violence to the solar system. The results of scientific technology are taken for granted, but the theories which lie behind them are not very widely understood, nor is their influence strong enough to prevent many people from holding beliefs which are inconsistent with them. Science is regarded as magic, with the result both that no limit is set in the popular imagination to the possibilities of travelling in space or even in time, and that occult theories and practices, however full of gibberish, are treated as serious rivals to it.

[18] *OC*, 108.

If the measure of certainty is thoroughgoing acceptance, in a way which requires not only that one assents to a theory but that one holds fast to its consequences, then scientific theories are not so very certain.

What of Wittgenstein's other examples? Should I really feel that everything was being plunged into chaos if I found myself doubting whether the person sitting beside me was my old friend Professor W? The idea, presumably, is not just that I forget his name, which happens easily enough as one gets older, even in the case of people one knows very well, but that I am not sure whether the descriptions which I believe my friend to satisfy really are satisfied by the man beside me. Well, it is not hard to imagine circumstances in which I might be deceived. My friend might have a twin brother of whom I had never heard; he might have hired an actor to impersonate him. It is unlikely that the impersonation would be so good as to deceive me for very long, but it is not inconceivable. This is, however, only an isolated case. I cannot seriously envisage my being mistaken in this way about the identities of all my friends, of my own wife and children. But suppose that the persons whom I so identified were all to assure me that I was mistaken, I should suspect that they were playing a cruel practical joke on me, or that I had lost my sanity, or perhaps that I was having a bad dream.

But might not this be a dream? Might I not be dreaming that these are my friends: might I not wake up to find that my whole environment was really quite different from what it now seems to me to be? Wittgenstein deals very summarily with this sort of doubt. 'The argument "I may be dreaming" ', he says, 'is senseless for this reason: if I am dreaming, this remark is being dreamed as well – and indeed it is also being dreamed that these words have any meaning.'[19] Again, later on, after claiming that he cannot be mistaken about his own name, he says 'But suppose someone produced the scruple: what if I suddenly as it were woke up, and said "Just think, I've been imagining I was called L. W.!" – well, who says that I don't wake up once again and call *this* an extraordinary fancy, and so on.'[20] And finally, having said that 'If someone believes that he has flown from America to England in the last few days, then, I believe, he cannot be making a *mistake*. And just the same if someone says that he is at this moment sitting at a

[19] *OC*, 383.   [20] *OC*, 642.

table and writing',[21] he goes on ' "But even if in such cases I can't be mistaken, isn't it possible that I am drugged?" If I am and the drug has taken away my consciousness, then I am not now really talking and thinking. I cannot seriously suppose that I am at this moment dreaming. Someone who, dreaming, says "I am dreaming", even if he speaks audibly in doing so, is no more right than if he said in his dream "it is raining", while it was in fact raining. Even if his dream were actually connected with the noise of the rain.'[22]

How good are these arguments? Let us examine them. For the proposition 'I truly believe that p' to be true, it is necessary and sufficient that 'p' be true and that I also believe it. Suppose that 'p' is the proposition 'I am dreaming'. In the cases that Wittgenstein envisages, this is true *ex hypothesi*. Consequently, if he refuses to allow that I can truly believe that I am dreaming, it must be because he assumes that the fact that I am dreaming makes it impossible for me to believe that I am. Indeed, he seems to go further. The implication of his example of the rain appears to be that so long as one is dreaming one cannot be credited with any occurrent belief. But why should this be so? Why should the fact that I am in the physical state of sleep, and that I show no signs of being conscious of what is going on around me, be taken to entail that I am not having any thoughts which can properly be characterized as either true or false? I can see no good reason for this view. If my memories of my waking reveries are taken at their face value, I see no reason why the same should not apply to my memories of my dreams. And if these memories are taken at their face value, then it will follow that I did have such and such thoughts while I was asleep and that I attached the same meaning to the words in which I formulated those thoughts as I attach to the words in which I express my recollections of them. I shall, indeed, have dreamed that these words were meaningful, but this does not exclude their really having been so. It would exclude it only on the assumption that everything that is dreamed is false. But this surely is itself a false assumption, and one that the sceptic does not require. It is sufficient for his purpose that the stories which we tell ourselves in dreams be false in the main, not that they be false in every detail. An analogy may be drawn here with works of fiction, which are not debarred from containing some true statements. A work of fiction of which the action is set in London does not cease to

[21] *OC*, 675.   [22] *OC*, 676.

be such because the topography of London is accurately represented in it. In dreams, such accuracy is seldom maintained, but there is no logical reason why it should not be. Indeed, it does not appear to be logically necessary that a dream should be false in any particular. For example, it is related of one of the Dukes of Devonshire that he dreamed that he was speaking in the House of Lords and awoke to find that he really was speaking in the House of Lords. Even if this story is untrue, it does not appear to be self-contradictory.

If the story is not self-contradictory, it is because to say that the Duke was dreaming that he was making a speech can be construed as saying no more than that the impression that he was making a speech was one that came to him while he was asleep. He was mistaken only in believing himself to be awake or at least in his failure to realize that he was not awake. This is, however, by all odds an exceptional case. The hold of dreams upon reality, in any straightforward sense, is sufficiently weak for the expression 'I must be dreaming' to mean much the same as 'This cannot really be happening'. It is, indeed, on this that the sceptic trades. But now we come to Wittgenstein's remaining argument. If the possibility that I am dreaming is to be one that I take seriously enough for it to make me uncertain whether my present experiences really are veridical, I must envisage myself waking to find that this has been only a dream. But then why should I take the experience of waking to be veridical? Why should not *that* be part of a dream and *this* the reality?

The answer to this is that if I seriously believe that I am now dreaming I must look forward to an experience of waking which I shall in fact take to be veridical. I shall, indeed, have no proof that it is veridical except that it coheres with the experiences that follow it and with what I take to be my memories of previous waking experiences, and that it is not itself followed by an experience of waking, which leads me to take it and its successors as being themselves the content of a dream. And then the same risk will be run by *this* experience. Thus my assessment of my current experience, whether I judge that it is or that it is not veridical, is never conclusive. It is open to revision in the light of further experience; and this further experience will be open to revision in its turn.

But this practically concedes Wittgenstein's point. We can, indeed, protest that the argument 'I may be dreaming' is not senseless, not only on the merely formal ground that it could logically be the case that I am dreaming, but also because the expectation which does occur in dreams, of waking up to find that one has been dreaming, has sometimes been fulfilled. The fact remains, however, that I do not now have this expectation, neither is there anything in the character of my present experience to give me any reason to have it. It is logically possible that in a few minutes time it will seem to me that I am waking from a dream, but I have no present ground for believing that this experience, even if it occurs, will have more authority as an indication of what is really taking place than those that I am having now. In short, the words 'I may be dreaming' are not under these conditions the expression of a serious doubt. It is as if I were to say 'All this may be an illusion' without having any better answer to the question 'What makes you think so?' than the formal point that since my interpretation of my present experiences makes some demands upon the future it is logically possible that it will not be substantiated.

Except that he at times appears unwilling to make even this logical admission, the nerve of Wittgenstein's argument is the requirement that doubt be serious; and the condition of its being serious is that it be capable of being resolved. Returning to the example of seeing colour, he maintains that to the question 'Can you be mistaken about this colour's being called "green" in English?', his answer can only be 'No'. 'If I were to say "Yes, for there is always the possibility of a delusion", that would mean nothing at all.'[23] 'But does that mean', he continues, 'that it is unthinkable that the word "green" should have been produced here by a slip of the tongue or a momentary confusion? Don't we know of such cases? – One can also say to someone "Mightn't you perhaps have made a slip?" That amounts to: "Think about it again". – But these rules of caution only make sense if they come to an end somewhere. A doubt without an end is not even a doubt.'[24] Similarly, he remarks that 'Only in certain cases is it possible to make an investigation "Is that really a hand?" (or "my hand"). For "I doubt whether this is really my (or a) hand" makes no sense without some more precise determination. One cannot tell from these words alone whether any doubt at all is meant – nor what kind of doubt.'[25] This follows a passage in which he has argued that our customary use of words like 'hand' without any doubt as to their meaning 'shows that absence of

---

[23] *OC*, 624.   [24] *OC*, 625.   [25] *OC*, 372.

doubt belongs to the essence of the language-game, that the question "How do I know?" drags out the language-game, or else does away with it'.[26]

From this point of view, it does not much matter whether we accept propositions like 'This is a hand' without further ado or whether we allow the question 'How do you know?' to divert us from propositions of this sort to propositions about sense-qualia. There is a philosophical interest in elaborating a 'language of appearances', because it helps us to realize how large an element of theory is already contained in our references to physical objects, and also makes it easier to exhibit the features of our sense-experiences on which the theory principally trades. So long, however, as we are operating within the theory, the margin which is allowed for error, though always present, is vanishingly small. There are standard tests for deciding whether or not we have identified an object correctly, or whether we are suffering some more radical illusion. When these tests have been carried out, the question is settled one way or the other: no provision is made for any further uncertainty. To go on to doubt the results of the tests, or indeed even to apply them when there is no special reason for thinking that anything is amiss, is to violate the principles on which the theory operates; in Wittgenstein's idiom, it is not to play the game. There is, indeed, always the logical possibility that future experiences will lead us to revise our beliefs in ways that we cannot now foresee, but it is part of our procedure not to take this possibility seriously, in any given instance, so long as it is merely formal: that is to say, so long as we have no positive reason for expecting it to be realized.

This might be thought to be a sufficient answer to the philosophical sceptic if his doubts were directed upon particular matters of fact. The truth is, however, that they are of quite a different character. They are not intended to make us more cautious in assuming that we know our own names or that we are using colour-words correctly, or that we were not born yesterday, or that we see with our eyes, or that we can identify our hands. A follower of Berkeley, who denies that there are physical objects, is not suggesting that the criteria which we use for determining the existence of such things as trees, or stars, or tables, or human bodies will not continue to be satisfied. He does not suppose that his own experiences are generally unlike those

[26] *OC*, 370.

of other people, or that they will be very different in the future from what they have been in the past. His peculiarity is that he wishes to interpret the evidence in a different fashion. He refuses to make the assumption that anything other than a spiritual substance is capable of existing unperceived.

But then is he not simply wrong on a question of empirical fact? If propositions of the sorts that Moore lists in his defence of common sense are in very many cases true, it follows automatically that a great many things which are not spiritual substances can exist unperceived; the trees in my garden, for example, the furniture in this room, and countless other physical objects of these and other kinds. It is true that Berkeley thought it possible to maintain both that there were trees and stars and tables and human bodies and whatever, and that there were no such things as physical objects, but here he was surely mistaken. If the words 'tree' and 'table' and all the rest of them are given their ordinary meanings, his position is self-contradictory.

The answer to this is that Berkeley would indeed be simply wrong if his denial of the existence of physical objects were put forward under the covering of the common-sense theory, which provides for their existence. But to treat his position in this way entirely fails to do it justice. So far from accepting the common-sense theory, he sought to overthrow it. His contention was not that the existence of things at times when they were not perceived was a possibility which happened not to be realized but that it ought not to be admitted as a possibility. He opted for a radically different way of interpreting experiences, in which this realistic assumption had no place. Consequently, Moore's and Wittgenstein's certainties do not touch him. For the doubts which they counter bear only upon the question whether the criteria which we use for determining the presence of physical objects are ever sufficiently satisfied: they have nothing to do with the question of modifying or replacing the criteria themselves. This is not to say that Berkeley or any other philosopher who has rejected the common-sense view has been successful in showing that the principles which furnish its theoretical background are logically defective, though even this needs to be proved by a rebuttal of these philosophers' arguments, rather than by a simple declaration of fidelity to common sense. The fact remains that whether or not there is anything wrong with our ordinary method of interpreting experience, the possibility of there being other workable methods is not excluded, as Wittgenstein indeed implicitly admits.

It is not even clear, without argument, that a view like Berkeley's cannot be taken of the theory with which we actually operate. Berkeley himself maintained that he was upholding the outlook of common sense against the false sophistication of a materialist philosophy, and although I believe that he was mistaken on this point, it is a question that is not settled by allowing Moore's claims to knowledge. The reason why it is not settled is that while Moore was wholly certain of the truth of the propositions which he enumerated he was not at all certain of their correct analysis. He did not know, and did not believe that anybody else knew, whether his seeing his hand consisted in the fact that some sense-datum was identical with part of the surface of his hand, or in the fact that the sense-datum stood in a causal or some other relation to a set of physical particles which were not themselves directly perceptible, or in the fact that the sense-datum was related in such and such ways to other actual and possible sense-data. The one thing he was sure of was that in expressing a proposition like 'This is a hand' one was saying something about a sense-datum, although other philosophers who have been equally certain of the truth of his examples have denied that sense-data come into it at all. But if there is so much uncertainty about what we know when we know such propositions to be true, the assurance that they are true does not amount to much.

This might be taken as support for Wittgenstein's argument that nothing useful is achieved merely by making claims to the possession of knowledge. But Wittgenstein's own attributions of certainty are open to the same objection. He gives many examples of propositions which he takes to be unquestionably true, but he does not say how any of them should be analysed. He may, indeed, have held that none of them stood in any need of analysis, but this at least is open to question. For instance, there is a long-standing problem with regard to the relation of common-sense propositions about physical objects to the propositions which figure in scientific theory. Are electrons and neutrons literally parts of the objects which we see? Are they logical fictions, which we introduce as explanatory tools? Or do they physically exist in a way that the objects in which common sense believes do not? Thus, Russell has argued that 'the coloured surface that I see when I look at a table has a spatial position in the space of my visual field; it exists only where eyes and nerves and brain exist to cause the energy of photons to undergo certain transformations. . . . The table as a physical object, consisting of electrons, positrons and neutrons, lies outside my experience, and if there is a space which contains both it and my perceptual space, then in that space the table must be wholly external to my perceptual space.'[27] If this were correct, the certainty of there being a table in front of me would come to no more than the certainty of the present occurrence of such and such percepts: all the rest would be a more or less hazardous conjecture. I do not say that it is correct. On the contrary, I think that there are insuperable objections to any theory which puts the constituents of physical space beyond the reach of our observation. But it is at least a serious attempt to dispose of a genuine problem. If we limit ourselves to saying that my acceptance of the proposition that there is a table in front of me is, in these circumstances, an obligatory move in the language-game that we ordinarily play then not only do we invite questions about the relation of this game to others that might be playable; we also leave room for differences of opinion as to what the game that we do play actually is.

I have spoken of our playing a language-game because this is an analogy that Wittgenstein frequently uses, but we need to consider how far it can be made to go. We do indeed modify our concepts on occasion in something like the way that we alter the rules of games, but we do not, antecedently to any use of language, decide what the rules are going to be. If we adhere to the analogy, we have to say that the language-game is one that is played before its rules are codified. This may be the point of Wittgenstein's remarking that 'the language-game is so to say unpredictable. I mean: it is not based on grounds. It is not reasonable (or unreasonable). It is there – like our life.'[28] He maintains also that it has its roots in action. 'Children', he says, 'do not learn that books exist, that armchairs exist, etc. etc. – they learn to fetch books, sit in armchairs, etc. etc.'[29] And in another passage, having argued that 'justifying the evidence comes to an end', he goes on to say that 'the end is not certain propositions' striking us immediately as true, i.e. it is not a kind of *seeing* on our part; it is our *acting*, which lies at the bottom of the language-game'.[30]

But our actions are conditioned by our beliefs, whether or not these beliefs are consciously formulated, and our beliefs, when we do

---

[27] *Human Knowledge: Its Scope and Limits* (Allen & Unwin), p. 236.
[28] *OC*, 559.   [29] *OC*, 476.   [30] *OC*, 204.

formulate them, are evinced by sentences which are intended to express what is true. When they fulfil this intention, it is for the most part not only because of the meaning of the words which they contain but also because things are as they describe them. So is not our use of language dependent not only on the rules of the game, but also, and indeed primarily, on the nature of things? Undoubtedly it is, but we have to remember also that what we count as the nature of things is itself not independent of the fashion in which we describe them. This is the point, or part of the point, of Quine's ontological relativity. Our judgements about what there is are always embedded in some theory. We can substitute one theory for another, but we cannot detach ourselves from theory altogether and see the world unclouded by any preconception of it. I do not know that Wittgenstein would have cared for this way of putting it, but the impossibility of there being any cognitive process which would require the prising of the world off language seems central to his position. It has now been discovered that Wittgenstein was influenced by Kant, and whatever objections there may be to Kant's idealism, his dictum that 'intuitions without concepts are blind' appears unassailable.

8　An Honest Ghost?

How radical is the central thesis of Ryle's *The Concept of Mind*? Would it be true to say that it denied the very existence of minds, in so far as their existence is understood to imply that there are 'inner' states or processes, or objects or events? There is, indeed, a great deal of evidence in the book that this is what Ryle intends. 'It is being maintained', he says, 'throughout this book that when we characterise people by mental predicates, we are not making untestable inferences to any ghostly processes occurring in streams of consciousness which we are debarred from visiting: we are describing the ways in which these people conduct parts of their predominantly public behaviour.'[1] Or again: 'The radical objection to the theory that minds must know what they are about, because mental happenings are by definition conscious, or metaphorically self-luminous, is that there are no such happenings: there are no occurrences taking place in a second-status world, since there is no such status and no such world and consequently no need for special modes of acquainting ourselves with the denizens of such a world.'[2] Or again: 'It has been argued from a number of directions that when we speak of a person's mind, we are not speaking of a second theatre of special-status incidents, but of certain ways in which some of the incidents of his one life are ordered. His life is not a double series of events taking place in different kinds of stuff; it is one concatenation of events, the differences between some and other classes of which largely consist in the applicability or inapplicability to them of logically different types of law-propositions and lawlike propositions. . . . So questions about the relations between a person and his mind, like those about the relations between a person's body and his mind are improper questions. They are improper in much the same way as is the question "What transactions go on between the House of Commons and the British Constitution?" '[3]

[1] Gilbert Ryle, *The Concept of Mind*, p. 51.
[2] p. 161.　　　[3] pp. 167–168.

It is in the same spirit that Ryle maintains that to explain an action is not to 'infer to occult causes' but to 'subsume under hypothetical and semi-hypothetical propositions', that 'the imputation of a motive for a particular action is not a causal inference to an unwitnessed event but the subsumption of an episode proposition under a law-like proposition';[4] that 'consciousness and introspection cannot be what they are officially described as being, since their supposed objects are myths';[5] and that while 'the concept of picturing, visualising or "seeing" is a proper and useful concept . . . its use does not entail the existence of pictures which we contemplate or the existence of a gallery in which such pictures are ephemerally suspended'.[6] All these and many similar passages suggest very strongly that the doctrine which Ryle is putting forward is a version of what is technically known as logical behaviourism. This is borne out by the fact that when he briefly discusses behaviourism in the concluding section of his book, the only serious fault that he finds with psychologists of this school is their tendency to combine a meritorious denial of ' "inner-life" occurrences' with what he regards as a mistaken addiction to Hobbist mechanism.

Nevertheless a closer reading of the book may make us wonder whether Ryle's position is quite so straightforward. For the programme of logical behaviourism to succeed, it has to be shown that all our talk about mental states and processes can be reformulated in such a way as to eliminate any reference to an inner life. In the version of the programme which we might attribute to Ryle, what would remain would be a set of dispositional statements about people's overt behaviour. 'To talk of a person's mind . . . is to talk of the person's abilities, liabilities and inclinations to do and undergo certain sorts of things, and of the doing and undergoing of these things in the ordinary world.'[7] The reasons for taking a view of this kind are commonly not that it is semantically plausible, but rather that it offers a way of escape from philosophical perplexities. It saves us from the difficulty, to which all dualistic theories are exposed, of explaining how mental and physical processes are related, or how one person can ever come to know what goes on in the mind of another. This is, indeed, a great advantage, but it has to be earned. The elimination of all the ostensible references that we make to inner occurrences has to be carried through.

[4] p. 90.   [5] p. 155.   [6] p. 247.   [7] p. 199.

Ryle does take it quite a long distance. He has arguments to show that displays of intelligence, whether in speech or action, do not entail private planning, that to exercise the will is not to engage in mental acts of volition, that motives are not 'ghostly thrusts', that neither perceiving nor imagining entails the awareness of private objects. He does not, however, take it all the way. There are many passages in his book in which a reference to what would appear to be inner occurrences is still permitted to remain. Thus, in the course of making out his distinction between knowing how and knowing that, he remarks that 'much of our ordinary thinking is conducted in internal monologue or silent soliloquy, usually accompanied by an internal cinematograph-show of visual imagery'[8] and he says of the exercises of knowing how that they 'can be overt or covert, deeds performed or deeds imagined, words spoken aloud or words heard in one's head, pictures painted on canvas or pictures in the mind's eye'.[9] He recognizes a special sense of the words 'mental' and 'mind', in which 'a boy is said to be doing mental arithmetic' when he says numerical symbols to himself 'performing his calculations in silent soliloquy', or 'a person is said to be reading the mind of another when he describes truly what the other is saying or picturing to himself in auditory or visual images'.[10] He does, indeed, go on to say that 'this special use of "mental" and "mind" in which they signify what is done "in one's head" cannot be used as evidence for the dogma of the ghost in the machine'.[11] The secrecy which we secure for our thinking by conducting it in auditory word-images 'is not the secrecy ascribed to the postulated episodes of the ghostly shadow-world. It is merely the convenient privacy which characterises the tunes that run in my head and the things that I see in my mind's eye.'[12] But, whatever may be the differences between these sorts of secrecy, the existence of inner processes appears in any case to be conceded.

In one significant passage, an admission of this kind immediately follows what might otherwise be taken to be its denial. Ryle has been arguing that the assumption, made by historians and scholars, that the qualities of people's minds are reflected in the things they say and do is only 'on the edge of the truth'. The truth is that 'the styles and procedures of people's activities *are* the way their minds work'; they are not reflections of any 'postulated secret processes'. So

---

[8] p. 27.   [9] p. 47.   [10] p. 34.
[11] p. 35.   [12] Ibid.

'Boswell described Johnson's mind when he described how he wrote, talked, ate, fidgeted and fumed.' But it would seem not entirely, for Ryle immediately goes on: 'His description was, of course, incomplete, since there were notoriously some thoughts which Johnson kept carefully to himself and there must have been many dreams, daydreams and silent babblings which only Johnson could have recorded and only a James Joyce would wish him to have recorded.'[13] Whatever we may think of the implications that the stream of consciousness which Joyce attempted to reproduce is not worth transcribing, there is also the implication that it is there to be transcribed.

A further admission is that of the existence of feelings, which Ryle equates with 'the sorts of things which people often describe as thrills, twinges, pangs, throbs, wrenches, itches, prickings, chills, glows, loads, qualms, hankerings, curdlings, sinkings, tensions, gnawings and shocks'.[14] As his choice of language indicates, he comes near to identifying feelings with bodily sensations, though he thinks that our descriptions of feelings may be metaphorical in a way that our descriptions of bodily sensations are not. He maintains that there are some feelings which we are ready to locate in particular parts of the body, as, for example, 'the sinking feeling of despair in the pit of the stomach', and of others, like glows of pride, which are not specifically located, he says that they 'seem to pervade the whole body in much the same way as do glows of warmth'.[15] All this is no doubt intended to take away from the 'mentality' of feelings, but the fact remains that they are allowed to be felt. There is no suggestion that talk of what a person feels, in this sense, can be translated into talk of the ways in which he is disposed to behave.

It may be unfair to add visual, auditory, and other perceptual sensations to the list of inner occurrences which Ryle apparently admits, since it would appear from the postscript to his chapter on 'Sensation and Observation' that he came to think that he had been mistaken in accepting the conventional view that perceiving entailed having sensations of these sorts. In the same way, the references to visual and auditory images, which we have found him making in the earlier part of his book, ought perhaps to be discounted on the ground that when at a later stage he writes about Imagination, he argues that 'seeing things in one's mind's eye does not involve either

[13] pp. 58–9.   [14] pp. 83–4.   [15] p. 84.

the existence of things seen or the occurrence of acts of seeing them.'[16] Even so, we are still left with what Ryle describes as fancying that one sees or hears things, as well as with seeing, hearing, and the other forms of perception themselves. Ryle does not explain what he takes fancying to be, apart from its not consisting in observing images, but if it is to do the work that he assigns to it, it would seem that it must be a mental state or process of some sort, and one for which no analysis is given in behavioural terms. Admittedly, Ryle argues that the various forms of sense-perception are not mental states or processes, since they are not states or processes at all. His ground for this is that verbs like 'see' and 'hear' are what he calls achievement words: like the words 'win' or 'cure' or 'discover' they are not used to describe any activity but rather to state that something has been brought off, some task accomplished, some process carried to fulfilment. I am not entirely convinced that this is so, but even if it were so, it would make little difference to the present argument. For now we have to ask what are supposed to be the processes of which seeing and hearing and the other modes of perception are the fulfilment. In the case of sight and hearing, the words 'looking' and 'listening' can be called into play: when it comes to the other senses, we shall probably be forced into circumlocution, unless words like 'touching', 'smelling', and 'tasting' are made to do double duty. But whatever words we use to stand for them, these processes cannot on the face of it be taken to be purely physical. If it is to be related to seeing as running in a race is related to winning it, looking at an object must imply more than having one's eyes in such and such a physical relation to it. In old-fashioned terms, looking and listening must be conscious processes. At any rate Ryle gives us no reason to think otherwise. He does not take the desperate course, which has been followed by some contemporary materialists, of trying to identify seeing and hearing with the acquisition of true beliefs, themselves reduced to behavioural dispositions, in consequence of the stimulation of the relevant sense-organs. However dissatisfied he may be with the standard philosophical accounts of sense-perception, he does not go to the length of dispensing altogether with any form of sentience.

What then are we to make of these mental residues: the silent soliloquies, the itches, pangs, and gnawings, the dreams and day-

---

[16] p. 245.

dreams, the processes of fancying, and those of which the various modes of perception are the achievements? Taken together, do they not furnish quite a robust inner life? How can Ryle admit them and yet not be haunted by 'the ghost in the machine'?

Though he would not care to have it put in these terms, the answer may be that he believes his ghost to be an honest ghost. It would, therefore, have to differ in some vital respect from the ghost which represents 'the official doctrine'; and the way in which he may think that it differs is that it does not command the stage of a private theatre. The inner occurrences which he is prepared to tolerate are not 'proprietary' in the way that the denizens of the mind have commonly been thought to be.

One difficulty at this point is that Ryle does not go into the question of privacy in any detail. There are, however, indications that the type of privacy to which he objects is that which is ascribed to occurrences, or objects, or states, or processes, of which it is held to be characteristic that the person to whom they are private observes them and that it is logically impossible that they should be observed by anyone else. He wishes to say that nothing is private in this sense.

Does he succeed in showing that the inner life to which I have argued that he is still committed does not have this forbidden type of privacy? In the case of sensations and feelings, the argument on which he relies is that, so far as the power of observation goes, there is no asymmetry between oneself and other people. 'It is true', he says, 'that the cobbler cannot witness the tweaks that I feel when the shoe pinches. But it is false that I witness them. The reason why my tweaks cannot be witnessed by him is not that some Iron Curtain prevents them from being witnessed by anyone save myself but that they are not the sort of things of which it makes sense to say that they are witnessed or unwitnessed at all, even by me. I feel or have the tweaks, but I do not discover or peer at them; they are not things that I find out about by watching them, listening to them, or savouring them. In the sense in which a person may be said to have had a robin under observation, it would be nonsense to say that he had had a twinge under observation. There may be one or several witnesses of a road-accident: there cannot be several witnesses, or even one witness, of a qualm.'[17] Of course there is still the difference that I feel this particular twinge and the cobbler cannot, but Ryle

[17] p. 205.

maintains that this is no more than a trivial point of logic. Another person cannot feel my twinges for the same reason that he cannot smile my smile or run my race or die my death. It is just that we are concerned here with cognate accusatives.

I am not convinced by this argument. The only reason which Ryle gives for saying that one cannot observe or witness one's sensations is that epithets which can be coupled with words like 'observing' and 'witnessing', when these are construed as task-words, cannot be applied to having sensations. We can be more or less successful at observing but not at having sensations, we can be said to observe, but not to have sensations, carefully or systematically, we can have motives for observing but not for having sensations, we can make mistakes of observation, but not of sensation, and so forth.[18] But the most that this proves is that having sensations is not engaging in a task. It is not doing research, though research may lead to it. But, if we are to believe Ryle, exactly the same is true of seeing, hearing, touching, and the other modes of perception. All his grammatical points apply just as well to them. Yet surely he would not wish to say that we do not observe or witness what we see.

The truth is that verbs like 'observe' and 'witness' are commonly used both as task-words and as achievement-words. If Ryle is to capitalize on the fact that not everything that can be said about observing can also be said about having sensations, he will therefore have to maintain that it is only when construed as a task that observing is cognitive. But then he will be mistaken. The parallel case of seeing is a sufficient counterexample.

There remains the point that sensations are cognate to feeling, whereas the objects which we perceive are not cognate to our perceiving them: from which it is inferred that the difference between perceiving and having sensations is not that one is acquainted with public objects in the one case and private objects in the other, but that while we can properly speak of there being objects of perception, to have a sensation is not to be acquainted with any object at all. My own view, about which I shall say a little more later on, is that this is a matter of policy. We are not bound to treat sensations, or feelings, or for that matter images, as private objects, but there is no compelling reason why we should not do so if we wish. But, however this may be, even if we rule out private objects, it

[18] *Vide* p. 204.

still will not follow, as Ryle assumes, that feeling is not a privileged source of information. The sense in which it is privileged can be illustrated by returning to Ryle's example of the ill-fitting shoe. No doubt the cobbler has ways of knowing that I feel the tweaks, although the sceptical arguments which put this assumption in question still have to be met: but only I know that the tweaks are being felt, on the basis of feeling them. It is for this reason and not, as has sometimes been suggested, because it is improper to credit a person with knowledge of his own sensations, that the question how do I know that I feel the tweaks is not appropriate, though it would be appropriate to ask any other person how he knew that I felt them. This point is in fact conceded by Ryle, when he sanctions the dialogue 'How do you know that the pain is in your leg and not in your shoulder?' 'They are my leg and shoulder aren't they?'[19] This need not imply that I cannot be mistaken with regard to such things as the location of my pains, but surely it is a claim, and a valid claim, to the possession of what Ryle calls 'privileged access'.

Much the same considerations apply to the cases of imagining and perceiving. It is not enough for Ryle's purposes to do away with mental images and sense-data. The fact that I am imagining or ostensibly perceiving whatever it may be will be known to me in a way that it cannot be known to other people. On the assumption that the objects of sense-perception are public, if they exist at all, I am not in a privileged position with respect to the identification of what I perceive: there are, however, the same reasons as in the case of my sensations for holding that I am in a privileged position with respect to knowing what it seems to me that I perceive, and my use a moment ago of the artificial expression 'ostensibly perceiving' was intended to make this qualification. In the case of imagining, the parallel with having sensations is obvious and Ryle indeed concedes it when, in a passage which I have already quoted, he speaks of Dr Johnson's day-dreams as something that only Johnson could record.

A point to which Ryle attaches some importance is that such records are retrospective. He rejects the theory according to which 'mental processes are conscious, not in the sense that we do or could report on them *post mortem*, but in the sense that their intimations of their own occurrences are properties of those occurrences and so are not posterior to them'.[20] He denies not only that mental processes, if

19 p. 239.   20 p. 160.

they existed, could be self-luminous but also that there could be such a thing as introspection, if this is taken to be a species of perception which has internal rather than external objects. His main argument against the view that mental processes are self-luminous is that the consciousness of a mental process cannot be identical with the mental process itself. For example, if the process is one of carrying out an inference, then 'my consciousness is of a process of inferring, but my inferring is, perhaps, of a geometrical conclusion from geometrical premisses. The verbal expression of my inference might be, "because this is an equilateral triangle, therefore each angle is 60 degrees", but the verbal expression of what I am conscious of might be "Here I am deducing such and such from so and so".'[21] In the same way, my consciousness of my consciousness of my process of inferring must be differentiated from my consciousness of the process. But then, if we take every mental process to be self-luminous we are led into an infinite regress. One might have expected Ryle to argue that a similar regress would arise on the assumption that every mental process was introspective, but he contents himself instead with the empirical arguments that there must be 'some limit to the number of possible synchronous acts of attention'[22] and that, as Hume pointed out, there are some states of mind which put us into too much agitation for it to be possible for us to scrutinize them coolly. These last objections do not apply to retrospection which, in Ryle's opinion, achieves all the legitimate ends for which introspection was thought to be required. Of course, retrospection is not infallible, as introspection has sometimes been taken to be: but the quest for infallibility is anyhow mistaken.

These arguments are not very easy to evaluate. What they seem to me to prove is first that the metaphor of the inner searchlight is not felicitous and, secondly, that it cannot rightly be assumed that we always in fact know what our mental processes are. On the other hand, they do not prove that there are any mental processes which are such that we are not in a position to know that they are occurring: and, what is more important, they do not prove that we do not obtain this knowledge, when we have it, in a way that is not available to anybody else. Neither does it seem to me to matter very much whether the knowledge is acquired concurrently with the mental process to which it relates or a little subsequently to it. I

[21] p. 162.   [22] p. 165.

should have thought that in some cases it was concurrent and in others not. The important point, in either case, is that, although the knowledge can be shared with others, we alone obtain it on the basis of actually undergoing, or having just previously undergone, the experience in question.

Ryle admits it to be true and important that 'the objects of my retrospection are items in my autobiography',[23] but will not allow that there is anything 'intrinsically ghostly' about them. 'In the same way that I can catch myself day-dreaming, I can catch myself scratching: in the same way that I can catch myself engaged in a piece of silent soliloquy, I can catch myself saying something aloud.'[24] But this is to miss the point. The fact that I can 'catch myself' in the performance of physical as well as mental activities does not entail that when the object of retrospection is mental, my access to it is not privileged. All that it entails is that this does not follow merely from the fact that it is retrospective.

In general, Ryle's strategy is not so much to deny the existence of 'privileged access' as to represent it as marking a difference of degree and not a difference of kind. 'The superiority of the speaker's knowledge of what he is doing over that of the listener does not indicate that he has Privileged Access to facts of a type inevitably inaccessible to the listener, but only that he is in a very good position to know what the listener is often in a very poor position to know.'[25] So, when Ryle speaks of thinking as silent soliloquy, the suggestion is that what makes it impossible for others to eavesdrop on my unspoken thoughts is that they are pitched in too low a key: thinking without saying what we think is like whispering very softly; so softly that no one else can overhear you. And then one wonders whether there could not be some device by which these whisperings could be magnified. For example, if, like the behaviourist Dr Watson, one were to identify thoughts with movements of the larynx, one could look forward to the time when all such movements would be capable of being recorded and the thoughts which they represented read off from them. But this is not Ryle's position. He nowhere suggests that his silent soliloquies are to be equated with physiological states or processes: nor does he make any attempt to translate them into behavioural dispositions. But if they are not transmutable into physical terms, it may not be a contingent fact that only their author

[23] p. 161.　　　[24] p. 166.　　　[25] p. 179.

overhears them. It is, indeed, contingent that I keep certain thoughts to myself, instead of expressing them in writing or in speech: but given that I do keep them to myself, it is arguable that the possibility of any other person's listening in to them is logically excluded, since there is nothing that would count as his listening in.

To this it may be objected that while such argument may conform to our current usage, it still takes too narrow a view of the empirical possibilities. Whatever the technical difficulties, it is surely not inconceivable that a portion of my brain should be transplanted into another person's body: and if that were to happen, he might come to remember my thoughts in just the way that I myself remember them. Indeed, one might go further: it is imaginable that my brain should be so connected to another person's that he currently caught on to my mental processes in just the way that I do. Admittedly, such examples put a strain on our concept of personal identity. There could be circumstances in which we should find it more natural to say that I had been translated into another body than that another person shared my memories, let alone my present consciousness. On the other hand, there could be circumstances in which we should find it more natural to abandon the rule that the experiences which one can remember, or even those of which one can be currently aware, are necessarily one's own.

I think that these possibilities have to be admitted; and if we admit them we may have to allow that it is only a contingent fact that my experiences are accessible to me in a way that they are not accessible to anyone else. Nevertheless, there will still be a distinction between knowing about an experience on the basis of having it, or recollecting it, and knowing about it only on the basis of observing the bodily states or behaviour of the person whose experience it is; and there will still be grounds for holding that a claim to knowledge which is based on having the experience in question is authoritative in a way that a claim which is based only on observation cannot be.[26] Moreover, some at least of the sceptical arguments concerning the possibility of our having any knowledge of this kind on the basis of 'external' observation will still need to be met. I do not say that there is no way of meeting them, although I do not think that any satisfactory way has yet been found. This is a problem that is almost ignored by Ryle, no doubt because he sees

---

[26] Cf. my essay on 'Privacy' in *The Concept of a Person*, especially pp. 68–73.

himself as having undercut it. He would, indeed, be justified in this assumption if he had made good the thesis of logical behaviourism. I have, however, tried to show not only that he has not made it good, but that it is doubtful even if he holds it in any rigorous form.

In fact, I think that there are three general theses in *The Concept of Mind* which Ryle does not explicitly distinguish. The thesis which I have just suggested that he probably does not hold, though his programmatic statements often imply that he does, is that all our talk about the mind is translatable into talk about behaviour. If he does hold this thesis, the least that one can say is that he has left himself a great deal of work to do: we have seen that he makes a number of admissions, which appear to be inconsistent with it. There is, however, a weaker thesis which is consistently held throughout the book. This is the thesis that, whether or not the programme of logical behaviourism can be carried through in its entirety, it does give a correct account of a great deal of what is ordinarily classified as talk about the mind. In a great many instances in which a person is said to satisfy a 'mental' predicate, what is being said of him is not only, and perhaps not at all, that he is undergoing some inner process, but rather that he is exhibiting or disposed to exhibit a certain pattern of behaviour. This can apply to the ascription of intelligence, of motives and purposes, of voluntary actions, of emotions and moods, and of thoughts when they are overtly expressed.

This thesis is weaker than the other, in that it does not do away with inner processes altogether. What it does is to minimize their role. When someone acts intelligently, his movements may be preceded or accompanied by some inner planning, but they need not be; the silent thought is not necessary for the performance to be intelligent. Similarly, when I utter a meaningful sentence, it is possible, but not necessary, that I have already run through the sentence 'in my head'; even if no such inner process has taken place, the utterance will still be the expression of my thought. In the case of the will, Ryle takes the stronger line of denying that there are any inner acts to which 'willing' could be taken to refer; but his main point, here again, is that even if such acts of volition were to occur, their occurrence could not be necessary to make an action voluntary; for one thing, the assumption that they were necessary would lead to an infinite regress, since it would make sense to ask whether these acts were voluntary themselves. When it comes to motives Ryle is on

less sure ground, since his theory that 'the imputation of a motive
. . . is the subsumption of an episode proposition under a law-like
proposition'[27] applies only to standing motives, like vanity or
ambition, to which, indeed, he confines his examples: it does not
apply to the occurrent motives that one may have for doing
particular actions, like leaving early to catch a train. He could,
however, have argued that even when one is acting from an
occurrent motive, one need not, though one may, avow it oneself:
and even if one does avow it, the avowal may take the form of an
overt utterance. Finally, the case of emotions is different from the
others, since here the occurrence of some inner feeling, or at least a
bodily sensation, does seem to be essential: even so it can be argued
that the feeling plays a relatively minor part in the complex state of
affairs in which the emotion consists: the attendant behaviour and,
still more, the behavioural dispositions are what really count.

I am doubtful whether this is true of all emotions – it applies, for
example, to anger better than it does to sorrow – but even if the
emphasis is wrong in this case, the general thesis seems to me true
and important. There has been a tendency among philosophers to
assume that everything that commonly passes for the work of mind
consists in, or at least essentially involves, some inner process, and it
is useful to have this tendency corrected. It needed to be shown that
such things as intending, willing, understanding, desiring, exercising
intelligence, even thinking, in concrete instances, consist in nothing
more than the fact that the person of whom they are predicated is
behaving or is disposed to behave in such and such a fashion.
Nevertheless the scope of the thesis should not be overestimated. In
the areas which it covers, it establishes for the most part only that
the occurrence of inner processes is not essential for the application
of a given mental predicate, not that they do not occur at all; and
there are important areas of mental activity which it does not cover.
As a result, no doubt of his flirtation with the more radical thesis of
logical behaviourism, Ryle gives the impression of thinking that all
the mental operations that really matter are overt operations. For
any ordinary purpose, the residue is negligible. Only a James Joyce
would bother with it. But, as we have seen, the residue is far from
negligible. It includes a considerable part of the exercise of memory
and of the imagination, and it includes every form of sentience. Until

---

[27] *The Concept of Mind*, p. 80.

it is shown that perceiving can be analysed in behavioural terms, the erosion of the inner life, to which this second thesis tends, will remain seriously incomplete. As I said before, attempts have been made to bring perception into line, but I do not myself think that they have been, or are likely to be, successful.

The third thesis which I find in *The Concept of Mind* is weaker still. It is that our ordinary talk about the mind is open to what Quine calls regimentation.[28] We do not have to conceive of minds as substances, or indeed as entities of any kind. We do not have to admit thoughts, or feelings, or sensations, or mental images, or sense-data as objects. The only subjects to which mental predicates need to be ascribed are persons, and any particular mental object, like an image or a sense-datum, can be transformed into a way in which a person is affected, that is, into a state or process which is adjectival to him. So thought will be replaced by thinking, images by imagining, feelings by feeling, and sense-data by perceiving or seeming to perceive.

But what of the accusatives of these words? Ryle does not enter into the question in any detail but I think that his policy, except in the case of perception and feeling, would be to make them propositional. Not all thinking is straightforwardly 'thinking that', but with a little adjustment, such activities as wondering, musing, speculating, doubting, pondering, even dreaming, can be represented as being directed on to propositions. Without too much strain, the same can be made true of optative activities like wishing, hoping, fearing, desiring, seeking, and regretting: their object will be the proposition that such and such a state of affairs obtains or does not obtain. In spite of Ryle's efforts, the case of imagining remains more difficult. It is not easy to see how having an after-image can be represented as fancying that something is the case. To this extent, imagining comes closer to perceiving, in cases where the perception is delusive. In the cases where it is veridical, there is no problem. The objects which are perceived are physical entities, in the broad sense in which anything counts as physical if it is a real constituent of the external world. These objects will serve also in the delusive cases in which the infidelity of the perception consists in its making them appear other than they are. But what is to be said when the delusive perception is a total hallucination? This does not force the

[28] *Vide* W. V. Quine, *Word and Object*, ch. V.

admission of sense-data. We can talk of our seeming to perceive, or thinking that we perceive, physical entities which do not in fact exist. But what sort of objects are these? The case of feeling, except in the sense, which is not here in question, in which 'feeling' is roughly equivalent to 'touching', is different in that it is not possible to divide its objects into those which do and those which do not exist. The pang which is felt in a phantom limb has the same status, as an entity, as the pang which is felt in any actual part of the body. If this status is not to be that of an object, it seems that expressions which refer to feelings will have to be treated as cognate accusatives of the verbs which govern them. What this amounts to is that one refuses to license the existential inference from a proposition of the form '*A* has the feeling *f*' to a proposition of the form 'There is a feeling *f*, which *A* has'. I do not know that any good reason can be given for this prohibition, except that on grounds of economy or a taste for neatness, one decides to have only physical entities in one's ontology, but neither do I see any strong objection to it. The objection that one might raise would be epistemological. It might be argued that since 'feelings are first', in the sense that they are epistemologically prior to the persons to whom they are attributed, they have the better title to existence. I accept the premiss of this argument and have in the past accepted its conclusion, but I now think, for reasons which I have developed elsewhere,[29] that epistemological and ontological priority do not have to go together.

The same technique can be applied to images and to the objects of hallucinatory perception. One can simply refuse to license the inference from '*A* is having an image' to 'There is an image which *A* is having' and from '*A* perceives a non-existent physical entity' to 'There is a non-existent physical entity which *A* perceives.' But here there is more reason for disquiet. Even as the designates of cognate accusatives, non-existent physical entities have a disreputable air. A better course, it seems to me, would be to admit sense-data and treat them as cognate to perceptual acts. But if we admit sense-data at all, how can we resist admitting them in other cases of perception, including those that are veridical? The answer is that there is no call to resist. That a perceptual act always has a cognate object does not preclude its also having a real one: and the real object, when it exists, will be a physical entity.

[29] *Vide The Origins of Pragmatism*, pp. 329 ff.

Since this technique could also be applied to thoughts and to the possibly non-existent objects of optative acts, one may wonder what is gained by bringing in propositional accusatives. A motive for doing so might be that propositions are at least not mental objects, but this is not enough to make them respectable. We can indeed refuse to treat them as entities, but then it is not clear why they are to be preferred to the non-entities which they replace. There would, however, be a reason for preferring them if they were thought to be eliminable. The introduction of propositional accusatives would then be a stage in the process of getting rid of intentionality. Propositions would be replaced in their turn by sentences: and an account of the use and understanding of sentences would be given in behavioural terms. I am attracted by this programme, and think that it ought to be successful, but it meets with difficulties which have not, in my view, as yet been overcome.[30]

Failing the completion of a programme of this sort, the regimentation of mental discourse does not amount to very much. It comes down to little more than a decision not to say that such things as feelings, images, and sense-data exist, or at any rate not to allow them the status of entities. No doubt Ryle intended more than this. When he denied the existence of images or sense-data, he wanted to show not only that we were not bound to include such things in our ontology, but that we were not entitled to. This could be achieved either by deduction from some ontological theory, which would itself then need to be justified, or by showing that the concept of the type of entity in question was such that nothing answered to it. Though Ryle has a physicalist ontology in the background, and sometimes proceeds as though he had established it, the course which he mainly follows is the second. The argument on which he relies is that neither imagining nor sensing, as this term is used by sense-datum theorists, is a sort of observing; in the case of sensing, this is backed by the argument that if perceiving entailed sensing, and sensing were itself a sort of perceiving, an admission of sense-data would involve a vicious infinite regress. If 'observing' is taken here as a task-word, the main argument holds; but then, as we have seen, it proves nothing to the purpose. If, in accordance with the infinite regress argument, observing is equated with perceiving, the grounds for saying that imagining and sensing are not sorts of

---

[30] *The Origins of Pragmatism*, pp. 173 ff.

observing would be either that they are not the completion of activities like looking and listening, or that they do not have physical entities as their objects. But even on the dubious assumption that perceiving is always the completion of an activity, there is no good reason why this should be made a necessary condition for any conscious state to have an existent object: and the point that the objects of imagining and sensing would not be physical entities plainly begs the question. Neither is there anything in the infinite regress argument. The ground for bringing in sense-data is that our ordinary judgements of perception commit us to more than is contained in the experiences on which they are based.[31] The invocation of sense-data is intended to provide us with a way of describing the contents of the experiences, without incurring any further commitments. It is not universally agreed that it succeeds in this, but if, as I believe, it does succeed, it clearly does not entail that we have to go on reducing our commitments *ad infinitum*. There is no foothold here for the regress to begin.

I conclude that Ryle has not shown that we are not entitled to admit even sense-data as entities, but at most that we are not bound to do so. The decision not to admit them, together with other 'private' entities like images and feelings, does not require a denial of their legitimacy. I think it can be shown that even if one starts, epistemologically, from the neutral monist basis of sense-data, images, and feelings, it is still possible and indeed desirable to have a physicalist ontology.[32] This is, indeed, a much weaker result than one would get if one were able to prove that all mental states or processes were logically or even factually identical with physical ones, but here I doubt if anything better is obtainable. If there are any hopes for physicalism, they must lie in the attempt to establish factual identity. The belief in a logical identity is simpler and bolder, but I think it has become clear that it is false.

This is not necessarily a reproach to Ryle since we have seen that he does not attempt to carry the logical thesis all the way. In fact, I believe that he takes it about as far as it can legitimately go. Of the three theses that I have extracted from *The Concept of Mind*, it is only the second that yields a substantial result, the third, in the form in which it is true, being too weak to be of very much interest. In short,

[31] Cf. my article 'Has Austin Refuted the Sense-Datum Theory?', *Synthese* 17 (1967).
[32] *Vide The Origins of Pragmatism*, pp. 173 ff.

what Ryle has succeeded in doing is to reduce the empire of the mind over a considerable area. This is an important achievement, and one that is brilliantly effected, but it does not fulfil Ryle's professed intention of entirely exorcizing the ghost in the machine. The movements of the ghost have been curtailed but it still walks; and some of us are still haunted by it.

9   The Vienna Circle

It is characteristic of Viennese positivism, which played such an important role in the second quarter of this century that almost no subsequent work of any philosophical interest has been unaffected by it, that its origin at the turn of the century is chiefly to be ascribed to one who was professionally a physicist rather than a philosopher. This man was Ernst Mach, who lived from 1838 to 1916, and became a *Privatdozent* at the University of Vienna in 1863, the year he also published his first book, a compendium of *Physics for Doctors*, having previously published half-a-dozen articles, most of which already exemplified his lifelong interest in the interconnections of physics with psychology. Four years later, before he was thirty, he was appointed to a professorship at the Charles University in Prague, where he continued teaching experimental physics for the ensuing twenty-eight years. It was during this period that he published his two most important books entitled, in their English translations, *The Science of Mechanics* and *Contributions to the Analysis of Sensations*. They both appeared fairly late in his career, *The Science of Mechanics* originally in 1883 and the *Analysis of Sensations* in 1886, but they had been preceded by seven other books, principally on optics, acoustics, and scientific methodology, and by more than a hundred published articles.

In 1895, the University of Vienna decided to institute a third chair in philosophy and Ernst Mach accepted an invitation to become its first occupant, on condition that he was also allowed to give lectures on psychology. He himself chose the title of 'Professor of the History and Theory of the Inductive Sciences', a title which was changed by his successor, the famous physicist Ludwig Boltzmann, to 'Professor of Theoretical Physics and Natural Philosophy'. Boltzmann did not sympathize with Mach's philosophy of physics mainly because Mach denied the reality of atoms, and this change of title enabled him to claim that he had no predecessor, so that he was able to avoid the courtesy of paying any tribute to Mach in his inaugural lecture. This was in 1902. Mach had suffered a stroke in 1901 which obliged him to retire from the chair, but did not prevent him from writing four more books, of which the most important is one entitled, in English, *Knowledge and Error*, which appeared in 1905. It has recently been reissued as a volume in the splendid Vienna Circle collection which H. D. Reidel and Company are publishing.

Philosophically, Mach's views are very similar to those of the American pragmatist William James who in his own way was as gifted a writer as his even more famous younger brother, the novelist Henry James. The difference between their styles is just the opposite of what one might expect. Paradoxically, it is Henry, who writes with the careful qualifications and minute attention to detail that one might expect of a philosopher, and William, who carries the reader away with his humour and zest and the vividness of his imagery. William James, on holiday from Harvard, met Mach in Prague in 1882 and they took greatly to one another. Among other things, James explained Hegel to Mach. One wonders what he said, since he had a very strong distaste for Hegel's philosophy, but he may have enabled Mach to understand how that sort of monolithic idealism could be emotionally attractive to tender minds.

The philosophy which James and Mach shared was one that later came to be known as Neutral Monism. This was after it had been taken up by Bertrand Russell, who held it from 1914 when he published *Our Knowledge of the External World* until at least 1921 when he published *The Analysis of Mind*. Later he moved away from it in the direction of scientific realism. *The Analysis of Matter* which came out in 1927 marks the turning-point, though the old view never wholly lost its attraction for him, and he occasionally rather startlingly reverted to it. Its basic tenet is that neither mind nor matter is part of what Russell called the ultimate furniture of the world. Both are constructions out of neutral stuff – the raw material of experience – most often simply called experiences by James, sensations by Mach, and sensibilia by Russell. The first two terms are not happily chosen because they suggest a subordination of matter to mind, which was not intended. James called his theory 'Radical Empiricism' and Mach acknowledged the affinity of his views to the classical British empiricists of the seventeenth and eighteenth centuries, Locke, Berkeley, Hume – especially Hume. Indeed, if one treats Hume as an analyst rather than a sceptic, an approach for which there is virtually no historical warrant, but one that requires surprisingly little tampering with the text, one can make a neutral monist out of him.

The dominant idea is that the difference between mind and matter is not a difference in substance, a distinction between two different sorts of stuff, but a difference in the relations of the basic elements. One and the same experiential item, in virtue of its relations to other elements, is both a member of a class of such items which we call a physical object and a member of the series which constitutes some person's mental biography (the person himself being nothing but a fusion of two classes of these different sorts). The way it was supposed to work was vividly illustrated by William James. His example is that of a typical case of sense-perception, his reader's current perception of James's book and of the room in which he is sitting. Philosophers will be most likely to tell him that the physical objects, which he takes himself to be perceiving, are not directly presented to him; the immediate data of perception are subjective impressions to which it is inferred that external objects correspond. But the trouble with such theories, as James says, is 'that they violate the reader's sense of life, which knows no intervening mental image but seems to see the room and the book immediately just as they physically exist'.[1] And what is more, it is the reader here who is right and the philosophers who are wrong. The philosophers have gone wrong because they have not been able to see how it was possible 'that what is evidently one reality should be in two places at once, both in outer space and in a person's mind'.[2] This difficulty is removed once it is seen that the object's being in two different places is no more than a matter of its belonging to two different groups, or as James prefers to put it, two different processes. The processes are differentiated by their having partly different constituents and by differences in the ways their constituents are related.

James gives only a summary of the theory but it is attractive enough to be worth working out in detail. Unfortunately, like most attractive theories in philosophy, when you do try to work it out in detail, it turns out to be false. Neither Mach nor James nor Russell nor those who have worked on the theory since, including myself, have ever succeeded in specifying the relations which would have to

---

[1] *Essays in Radical Empiricism*, p. 12.   [2] Ibid., p. 11.

hold between the sensory elements for them to constitute on the one hand any sort of physical world and on the other a set of mental biographies. Nor, I am afraid, is it merely a matter of our incompetence. There are good reasons for concluding that such a programme cannot be carried through. I do however still believe – I am one of the very few philosophers nowadays who do – that one can defend a rather less ambitious theory along something the same lines.

But how, one may wonder, did a first-rate physicist like Mach come to adopt a theory of this type? How did he deal with atoms and electrons and quanta? He died too soon to be troubled with black holes and quarks but their arrival hasn't made the problem essentially different. The answer is that he took a pragmatic or operationalist view of physical theories. They were imaginative constructions, the point of which consisted in their providing you with a means of ordering your observable data and so enabling you to make successful inferences from one experimental situation to another. There was no need to suppose that the entities which figured in them really existed, any more than in applying mathematics, you need to postulate the reality of a Platonic world of numbers. This approach to physics has its difficulties, though Mach is not the only physicist to have adopted it. The fashion nowadays sets towards realism – but I think that the pragmatist view is still defensible.

Five years after Mach's death in 1916, his chair of the History and Philosophy of the Inductive Sciences was revived and Moritz Schlick was invited to occupy it. Schlick, who was born in 1882, was not an Austrian but a German and he too began as a physicist. His doctoral dissertation, which he completed at the University of Berlin in 1906, under the supervision of Max Planck, was about the reflection of light in a non-homogeneous medium. Though he retained an interest in physics – he wrote a paper on 'The Philosophical Significance of the Principle of Relativity' as early as 1915 and two years later a small book on 'Space and Time in Contemporary Physics' which drew praise from Einstein – he decided early on to pursue an academic career in philosophy rather than in physics and held professorships, first at Rostock and then at Kiel, before coming to Vienna. His philosophical interests were wide, embracing ethics and aesthetics as well as the philosophy of science and the theory of knowledge. Indeed the first book that he published in 1908 (one of the few of his works that has never been translated) was entitled *Lebensweisheit: Versuch einer Glückseligkeitslehre* and was, as the title indicates, concerned with the pursuit of happiness. But the book which made him famous and was probably responsible for his appointment to the Viennese chair was his *Allgemeine Erkenntnislehre* (*General Theory of Knowledge*) which he published in 1918, bringing out a second and considerably revised edition in 1925. Strangely, it was not until 1974 that it was translated into English.

By the time he published the second edition of this book Schlick had been converted to a view of science which was substantially the same as Mach's, and he had also come to think, again agreeing with Mach, that the basic statements of observation were statements about sense-data. In the original edition, he had adopted a more realistic standpoint. He insisted that every scientific statement or theory must be capable of being verified, in the sense that it had to have consequences which were capable of corresponding to observable facts, but the observable facts could have physical objects for their constituents. He agreed with Mach in rejecting psychophysical dualism, arguing that talking in mental or physical terms was just adopting one or other way of describing the same phenomena, but he tended to treat the phenomena as physical, in some degree anticipating the current fashion of identifying mental occurrences with processes in the central nervous system. This was another view which he was later to revise in favour of the Machian form of monism. Perhaps the most remarkable feature of Schlick's book was that he anticipated Wittgenstein, of whom he had not then heard, though he was later to come very much under Wittgenstein's influence, in rejecting Immanuel Kant's view that there could be such things as synthetic *a priori* truths, and holding that all true *a priori* propositions, such as those of logic and pure mathematics, were analytic – that is to say, true only in virtue of the meaning of the signs which were used to express them, and consequently devoid of any factual content.

Since Schlick held regular discussions with his philosophical and some of his scientific colleagues almost from the moment of his arrival in Vienna, it is difficult to assign a precise date to the institution of what came to be called the Vienna Circle – *Der Wiener Kreis* – over which Schlick presided for the remainder of his life, but I suppose as good a date as any would be the year 1924, two years before

Rudolf Carnap, one of the three leaders of the Circle (the third being Otto Neurath of whom I shall be speaking presently) came to Vienna.

A younger man than Schlick, having been born in 1891, Carnap was also a German and also worked on a doctoral dissertation on experimental physics, though he never completed it owing to the outbreak of the First World War in which he served as an officer in the German army. He obtained his doctorate at Jena in 1921 with a new dissertation on the topic of Space – subtitled a contribution to the Philosophy of Science. Like Schlick he had been struck by the philosophical importance of Einstein's Theory of Relativity and, with the exception of one pamphlet concerning the part played by the concept of simplicity in physics, and another on the different levels of the construction of physical concepts, the passage from the qualitative to the quantitative and from the concrete to the abstract, the half-dozen articles and pamphlets which he published before he came to Vienna were all devoted to the topics of Space, Time, and Causality. His view of physics was already less realistic than Schlick's then was, and closer to that of Mach. Later we shall see that their positions were reversed. Carnap had been an undergraduate at Jena and had been one of the very few students there to attend Gottlob Frege's courses on mathematical logic.

Frege, who lived from 1848 to 1925 and published his most important work from the 1870s to the 1890s, is now almost universally acknowledged to have been the greatest logician since Aristotle but he was almost totally unknown in Germany in his lifetime, and unappreciated even in his own university, where he never achieved the rank of full professor. Throughout one of his courses, given in 1913, there were only three persons in the audience, of whom Carnap was one. Frege's work was indeed known to Russell who discovered a contradiction in Frege's system, the possibility of constructing in it the famous class paradox – the class of classes which are not members of themselves being a member of itself, if it is not; and not being a member of itself if it is – and communicated it to Frege just before the publication of the second volume of Frege's *magnum opus* on the Foundations (*Grundgesetze*) of Arithmetic, a blow from which Frege never fully recovered.

Through Frege, Carnap learned of Russell's and Whitehead's *Principia Mathematica*, and went on to study Russell's works on the theory of knowledge, written during the period of Russell's neutral monism, and was very greatly influenced by them. Carnap had read the *Principia* when he was at Jena but did not possess a copy, and at the time of post-war German inflation could not afford to buy one. Nor could he borrow a copy from the library of the University of Freiburg, to which he had moved from Jena, since there was no copy there and never had been. He therefore applied to Russell who did not send him a copy but wrote Carnap a thirty-five-page letter, setting out all the most important definitions on which the proofs in the *Principia* were founded. This enabled Carnap to compile his *Abriss der Logistik* (*Outline of Mathematical Logic*) of which he wrote the first draft in 1924 though it was not published till 1929. It made him the first German philosopher, so far as I know, to take official notice of the expansion of logic, at least in its bearing on the foundations of mathematics, some fifty years after Frege had initiated it.

Upon his arrival in Vienna, Carnap set himself to complete the first of his major works *Der Logische Aufbau der Welt* (*The Logical Construction of the World*) which appeared in 1928. It also had to wait over forty years for an English translation. An exceedingly ambitious work, displaying, as all Carnap's work did, enormous industry and exceedingly high technical accomplishment, it adopted the standpoint of what Carnap called methodological solipsism. The word 'methodological' was put in to disinfect the solipsism, but it may be doubted whether it was sufficient for the purpose. Anyhow, Carnap, following Mach, James, and Russell after his own fashion, took as his starting-point the series of elements each constituting the whole of a person's current experience at a given moment, and attempted to show how the entire battery of concepts needed to describe the world could be constructed stage by stage, by the application of Russell's logic, on the basis of the single empirical relation of *Ahnlichkeitserinnerung* (remembered similarity). The higher levels of the construction, the development of physical objects and the constitution, out of a subclass of them, of other minds are sketched only in outline, and Carnap's ingenuity is mainly spent in showing how qualities like colours can be defined on the basis of the primitive relation in a purely structural extensional fashion. He did not succeed in this as was shown some thirty years later by Nelson Goodman, in his remarkable book *The Structure of Appearance*.

Carnap did not remain long in Vienna; he and another prominent member of the Circle, the physicist Philipp Frank, both left in 1931 to take up professorships at the Charles University in Prague; but he continued through his writings to exercise a predominant influence over the movement. In 1930, the Circle had taken over a journal called *Annalen der Philosophie*, renamed it *Erkenntnis*, and made it the chief outlet for the expression of their views, and Carnap continued to edit it in collaboration with Hans Reichenbach, another philosopher of physics, with a special interest in the theory of probability, who presided over a smaller group in Berlin. Carnap was also one of the three authors of the manifesto which the Circle published in 1929 under the title *Wissenschaftliche Weltauffassung – Der Wiener Kreis* (roughly translatable as *Viewing the World Scientifically – The Vienna Circle*). The other two authors were Hans Hahn, a professor of mathematics at Vienna University who died in 1934, and Otto Neurath, perhaps the strongest personality of them all, the most humorous and physically the largest; he used to sign his letters with a drawing of an elephant.

Neurath was not attached to the University of Vienna, but was the director of a Social and Economic Museum which he himself had founded in 1924. He had been born in Vienna in 1882 and educated at the Universities of Vienna and Berlin. He began by studying mathematics in Vienna, went on to linguistics, then to law, then to economics, and then to sociology. The thesis with which he obtained his doctorate in Berlin in 1906 was on the subject of the economic thought of the ancient world. The eighty articles which he published before the First World War were mainly concerned with economics but some of them were political, displaying a strong interest in the Balkans, especially Serbia and to a lesser extent Bulgaria (they included a short piece, for example, on the Bulgarian railway-system), and half a dozen of them were in the field of logic and mathematics. In the whole of his career he published only one substantial book, his *Empirische Sociologie* (*Empirical Sociology*) which came out in 1931, and appeared in an English translation in 1974, but over two hundred and seventy articles. After doing his military service in the Army Service Corps, in which he was to serve again, mainly in Galicia, during the war, he taught political economy at the New Vienna Academy of Commerce. He was not yet a socialist, though well schooled in the writings of Karl Marx and other socialist authors, but joined the Social Democratic party in 1918, partly as the result of his war experiences. He had ended the war as Director of the Museum for War Economy in Leipzig, being seconded from the Ministry of War in Vienna, and was appointed to a lectureship at Heidelberg in Max Weber's department of Sociology. He gave this up in order to serve the Socialist Government which had been set up in Bavaria with its headquarters in Munich, and was soon put in charge of its central planning. When this government was replaced by the so-called Spartacist government, consisting of Communists, left-wing Socialists, and Anarchists, working for once in some sort of cohesion, Neurath stayed on. This government was soon overthrown by the reactionary Freikorps, known like their unsuccessful counterparts in Russia as the White forces. Having narrowly escaped assassination by Count von Zeppelin, who subsequently made some sort of amends by marrying an American who translated Carnap's *Logische Syntax der Sprache* into English, Neurath was arrested and sentenced to eighteen-months imprisonment in a fortress. But the Austrian government intervened and the sentence was commuted to expulsion from Germany, and a seven-year ban on his returning there. He remained a Socialist and drew closer to Marxism, without, however, becoming a Communist. Nearly all the members of the Circle held left-wing views but the others did not bring them into their philosophy. Neurath alone saw the Circle as being in part a political movement. I shall have more later on to say about the subsequent course of his extraordinary career.

In the appendix to the manifesto the members of the Circle are listed as fourteen in number. Besides those already mentioned (Schlick, Carnap, Neurath, Frank, and Hahn), the Circle consisted of the philosophers Victor Kraft, Gustav Bergmann, Herbert Feigl, Marcel Natkin, Theodor Radaković, and Friedrich Waismann, and the mathematicians Karl Menger, Kurt Gödel, and Olga Hahn-Neurath (Hans Hahn's sister and Neurath's second wife). Bergmann and Feigl soon left to take up appointments in the United States and were replaced by Bela von Juhos and Edgar Zilsel, already mentioned in the manifesto as a sympathizer. The Circle was in close contact with Reichenbach's tiny group in Berlin, of which the most prominent members were Richard von Mises, like Reichenbach himself an ardent defender of the frequency theory of probability, the logician Kurt Grelling, and the young Carl Hempel, who was later to have an outstanding career in the United States, and with the more important group of Polish logicians and philosophers, of which the leading representatives were Łukasievicz Leśniewski, Chwistek, Kotarbinski, Ajdukiewicz, and Tarski. It was also on the look-out for what one might call likely prospects in other countries. It was, for example, my very good fortune that Schlick met my Oxford tutor Gilbert Ryle at an international congress held in England in 1930, with the result that two years later when I had taken my BA degree at Oxford and was allowed a few months leave of absence before starting work as a lecturer, Ryle advised me to go to Vienna. He gave me a letter of introduction to Schlick which I summoned up the courage to present, calling on Schlick in his handsome apartment in the Prinz Eugen Strasse. He spoke good English (he had an American wife) and made on me above all an impression of urbanity – like an American senator in a pre-war film. He graciously invited me not only to frequent the University but, what was much more important, to attend the meetings of the Circle. It was there that I first met Quine. I was just twenty-two and Quine a few years older – he had already taken his doctorate at Harvard. I remember his giving us a lecture – some sort of preliminary to his A System of Logistic. My own German was then too rudimentary for me to do more than vaguely follow what was being said, but I was helped by reading all of their publications that I could lay my hands on.

Apart from *Erkenntnis*, the most important source for what was going on in those early years, the Circle put out a series of monographs with the collective title of *Einheitswissenschaft* (Unified Science – this was a pet idea of Neurath's, not only that philosophy was to be annexed to science but that there was no difference in method between the natural and the social sciences) and a series of books, under the general editorship of Schlick and Philipp Frank, with the collective title of *Schriften zur Wissenschaftlichen Weltauffass-ung*. They included Neurath's *Empirische Sociologie*, a book by Schlick on Ethics, *Fragen der Ethik*, defending a form of utilitarianism, one by Frank on *The Law of Causality and its Limitations*, and Karl Popper's *Logik der Forschung* (translated into English over twenty years later as *The Logic of Scientific Discovery*). Popper, though teaching at a high school at Vienna at the time, was never admitted into the Circle (I don't know why – there may have been personal reasons) and has always exaggerated the differences between his views and theirs. There were differences, but only, in my opinion, of a minor character. I shall return to this briefly later on.

The first volume scheduled to appear in the series, continuing to be advertised as No. 1 even after the appearance of all the others,

was Waismann's *Logik, Sprache, Philosophie*, a title from which my
own *Language, Truth and Logic* was partly plagiarized. It never did
appear, mainly because of the debt which it would have owed to
Ludwig Wittgenstein. To explain this I shall have to say something
about Wittgenstein himself, apologizing to those for whom it is an
old story. Born in 1889, he came from a rich Viennese family – I
think they largely controlled the Austrian steel industry – and
studied engineering at Berlin. He then, like Engels before him, was
dispatched to Manchester, where he worked on aerodynamics. This
led him to take a deeper interest in mathematics and he became
aware of the work of Frege and Russell on mathematical logic. As a
result, he went to Cambridge in 1912 to study under Russell. There
is a story of his attending a course of Russell's lectures, never
saying a word but coming up to Russell at the end of the course and
saying: 'Either I am a genius or I join the Austrian air force,
which?' He looked a genius, but that was not quite enough for
Russell, so he asked Wittgenstein to submit him some written work.
When they met again at the beginning of the following term
Russell said: 'Don't join the air force.' After that they worked on
equal terms (if anything, Russell deferring to the much younger
Wittgenstein – Russell was born in 1872) until the war when
Wittgenstein fought for the Austrians – not as it turned out for
their air force but as a machine-gunner. He was captured by the
Italians, shortly before the Armistice, and was held as a prisoner of
war well into 1919.

Two important things happened to Wittgenstein during the war.
The first was that he decided, some say as a result of reading a work
of Tolstoy's, that it was wrong for him to be so rich and gave all his
money away. (A story which I have heard but do not vouch for is
that he did not give it to the poor, since that would corrupt them,
but to his sister who had a rich husband besides being rich in her
own right, so that a third fortune couldn't do her much harm.) The
second more important event was the completion of the only
philosophical book[3] he published in his lifetime – the famous
Logische-Philosophische Abhandlung – Tractatus Logico-Philosophicus in the
English version – which appeared as a lengthy article in the *Annalen*
in 1921, and was published in England in 1922 with the German text
and English translation by C. K. Ogden (part-author with I. A.

---

[3] The only other book that Wittgenstein himself ever published was a dictionary for
primary-school children: *Wörterbuch für Volksschulen*.

Richards of the *Meaning of Meaning* and the inventor of Basic English) on facing pages, with an introduction by Bertrand Russell.

In view of the very great influence of the *Tractatus*, almost immediately on the Vienna Circle and eventually on the younger generation of British philosophers, it is worth giving a very brief summary of its central ideas. They were that the world consists of what in the original translation were called atomic facts (*Sachverhalte* – a better rendering would have been states of affairs), which are logically independent of one another. These basic facts are mirrored by elementary propositions. To have any literal significance a sentence must express either a true or false elementary proposition or one that assigns a certain distribution of truth or falsehood to the elementary propositions. There are two limiting cases. A proposition may disagree with all the elementary truth-possibilities, in which case it is a contradiction, or it may agree with them all, in which case it is a tautology. The true propositions of logic were tautologies and so virtually were the propositions of mathematics, though Wittgenstein preferred to call them identities. They could be useful in inference but in themselves said nothing about the world. Anything else that failed to satisfy these conditions of meaning (and this included all transcendent discourse whether religious, moral, or metaphysical) was a pseudo-proposition – a piece of nonsense. This included philosophy too, which was not a body of doctrine but an activity, the activity of clarifying what could be said and preventing the expression of what couldn't. There was a mystical strain in Wittgenstein which led him to hint at the existence of things outside the reach of language. In some cases, such as the relation of language to the non-linguistic facts, what could not be said could be shown. This partly emerges in the formulation of the famous concluding sentence of the *Tractatus*: 'Wovon man nicht sprechen kann darüber muss man schweigen' – 'What we cannot speak about we must consign to silence' – provoking from Neurath the characteristically robust comment 'Mans muss ja schweigen aber nicht über etwas' – 'We must indeed be silent but not about anything'. A point still better put by Ramsey as 'What we can't say we can't say and we can't whistle it either.'[4]

After publishing the *Tractatus* Wittgenstein became a village schoolmaster at a place called Trattenbach in the mountains about

---

[4] *The Foundations of Mathematics*, p. 238.

sixty miles south of Vienna. The boys seemed to have liked him, though he was eventually accused of beating them too hard, but the villagers didn't, nor he them. He wrote to Russell that the men of Trattenbach were the wickedest in the world, a proposition which Russell found improbable. They did, however, succeed in making Wittgenstein's position at the school untenable, and he returned to Vienna to become an architect. I don't know that he ever collaborated on any building except a house for his sister which is now the Bulgarian Embassy. It was in the style of Gropius. About 1925 his interest in philosophy revived and he made contact with Schlick, Carnap, and Waismann. In 1929 he was persuaded to return to Cambridge as a Fellow of Trinity, succeeding G. E. Moore as a Professor in 1939 and holding the chair till ill health forced him to resign it two or three years before his death in 1951. Throughout the thirties he continued, however, to return to Vienna almost every summer. He quarrelled with Carnap over Carnap's *Aufbau* apparently on the score of plagiarism. Carnap had acknowledged his debt to him but this was taken as an aggravation of the offence. Wittgenstein is reported to have said: 'I don't mind a small boy's stealing my apples but I do mind his saying that I gave them to him.' He continued however to discuss philosophy with Schlick and Waismann, especially Waismann who was Schlick's assistant. The trouble was that Wittgenstein was changing his ideas. One can follow out the course of this change by reading the so-called Blue and Brown books, notes of his lectures dictated to his pupils and posthumously published, and find its fuller effects in Wittgenstein's posthumous *Philosophical Investigations*, which I am not going to try to summarize apart from saying that its main theme is that we fall into philosophical perplexity through misunderstanding the logic of our language, a thesis not proved but supported by a wealth of brilliant examples. Waismann's book was designed in part to reflect these changes. Wittgenstein was not opposed to this in principle but in fact prevented the book's appearance by insisting year after year on further revisions. The story ends sadly. When the Nazis invaded Austria in 1938 Waismann fled with his wife and son to Cambridge and was given a position there. But there was no place in Cambridge for an echo of Wittgenstein and Wittgenstein did not welcome him there. Fortunately Oxford took pity on him and made him a Reader in the Philosophy of Mathematics, a post which he held till his death in 1959. He suffered private misfortunes – both his wife and son committed suicide – and remained rather an isolated figure, but he went on working, mainly in his later years composing epigrams. His book was published posthumously and did turn out, to my mind at least, to owe too much to Wittgenstein's *Investigations*. The sad thing was that he was philosophically gifted in his own right. His book *An Introduction to Mathematical Thought* (first published in German in the thirties) and his series of articles in *Analysis* in the 1950s on Analytic–Synthetic are well-worth reading.

The original position of the Vienna Circle was very much that of Wittgenstein's *Tractatus*, on the assumption that Wittgenstein's elementary propositions were observational, except that the Circle did not adopt his pictorial theory of language. The points which they chiefly pressed were the subordination of philosophy to science – it could not compete with science because there *was* only the natural world which the sciences, with the support of observation for their theories, already wholly covered; all it could do was analyse the information which the sciences provided, perhaps do something more positive in the way of sharpening scientific concepts (functioning, in Carnap's phrase, as the logic of science) – and secondly, the exclusion of metaphysics – represented by any attempt to go beyond what Hume (in whose work almost the whole of Viennese positivism was foreshadowed) called matters of fact. This was effected by the use of their famous Principle of Verifiability – the slogan expressed by both Schlick and Waismann in the form 'The meaning of a proposition consists in its method of verification.'

It did not detract historically from the power of this slogan that it concealed many difficulties. For example, how strong was the verification to be? At the beginning, Schlick insisted on conclusive verification, but this threatened to rule out scientific generalizations; unless they were construed as finite conjunctions, which was not plausible, they could not be conclusively verified. It was on this point that Popper joined issue with the Circle, advocating a principle of Falsifiability and treating it not as a criterion of meaning but as a principle of demarcation. Only propositions which were falsifiable were to be accounted scientific. This proposition had its advantages but Popper actually defined falsifiability in such a way that it did not cover abstract theories, that is theories containing non-observational terms or even statements of probability as he construed them, not that in these respects his opponents were in any better case. Where he chiefly went wrong was in supposing that he had evaded Hume's problem of induction. It still needs to be explained why a hypothesis which we have tried and failed to falsify should gain credibility from passing the test.

Others, like Carnap, preferred to weaken the principle of verifiability by requiring no more than that empirical propositions should be confirmable. Unfortunately they didn't, and we still don't, have a watertight formal theory of confirmation, with the result that the principle of verifiability never got itself satisfactorily formalized. I made a valiant attempt to bring it off in the second edition of my *Language, Truth and Logic* but Alonzo Church torpedoed me.[5]

But worse is to come. The principle, as Schlick and Waismann stated it, fused two separate functions – that of deciding when a particular proposition was meaningful and that of deciding *what* meaning it had. The second was the more ambitious but it raised an awkward problem. Was it to be verifiability by the author or interpreter of the proposition? If so, its meaning would depend on who he happened to be and what spatio-temporal position he occupied, and we at once run into difficulties concerning propositions about the past (they have to be interpreted as propositions about the availability of present and future evidence), and propositions about other minds which have to be interpreted behaviouristically, a course which was later found to lead to an all-out behaviourism of, if not behaviourism, physicalism. By no means all philosophers object to this but it still seems to me to require one's feigning anaesthesia. The alternative was to rely on the fiction of an ideal observer, but this is not a very precise notion. With what powers is he to be credited?

There was disagreement also about the nature of *Protokolsätze*, the Circle's term for the basic observation-statements. Schlick and Waismann followed Mach in taking them to be sense-datum statements but Neurath, who won over Carnap, insisted that they must refer to the observation of physical objects. As I now recollect it, the discussion of this point occupied many of the Circle's sessions at which I assisted. Carnap was away in Prague but Schlick and Neurath battled it out, neither convincing the other. The advantage of Neurath's position was that he avoided a lot of awkward problems. But had he the right to? Schlick faced the problems but ran into difficulties – especially over the question of solipsism. How did he arrive at the public external world of which Neurath and

[5] In *The Journal of Symbolic Logic* (1949), pp. 52–3.

Carnap were making themselves a present? He eventually hit on the ingenious solution of construing public statements as statements about structure as opposed to content. It does not matter to me what the content of your experience is like, whether, if I could *per impossibile* get into your skin, I should or should not find that the world seemed very different, so long as I can cash your statements and your reactions to my statements in ways that make sense to me in terms of my own experience, and all that this requires is that our respective worlds have a structural correspondence. I once thought that this distinction between structure and content could not be so sharply drawn but I am now more inclined to think that there is a good deal in this idea.

Another disputed issue was that of the nature of truth. Schlick held some form of correspondence theory, but Neurath and Carnap maintained that to talk of comparing sentences with facts was metaphysical. Sentences could be compared only with other sentences. They were therefore driven to hold a coherence theory of truth. To the obvious objection that many incompatible systems of sentences could each be internally coherent, Carnap replied that the true one was that which was accepted by the scientists of our culture circle. But this, as I pointed out at the time, was a fudge. Each one of the competing systems might consistently contain the sentence that it alone was accepted by contemporary scientists. What Carnap meant was that only one of them was so accepted in *fact*. But why should it be only at this point that fact is allowed to intrude?

This outlawing of semantics, for that was what it came to, vitiated Carnap's *Logical Syntax of Language* which came out in Vienna in 1934 and was translated into English in 1937. Technically, it was a monumental feat, but the attempt to make syntax do the work of semantics failed and so did the construal of philosophical propositions, where they were not metaphysical, as syntactical statements masquerading as statements of fact (this was the nub of Carnap's celebrated distinction between the formal and material modes of speech). Whatever else they were, philosophical propositions were not syntactical.

Carnap's eyes were dramatically opened at a congress in Paris in 1935 when Tarski presented an abstract of his semantic theory of truth. Thereafter semantics became respectable and Carnap published three books on it between 1942 and 1947. The Circle had held previous congresses, two at Prague and one at Königsberg (though

it had no particular respect for Kant) but the Paris one was by far
the most ambitious. Bertrand Russell came to it and was treated as
an honoured figure, though he always held considerable reservations
about Logical Positivism. I don't remember meeting him then
though we became close friends in the years after the Second World
War. I do remember meeting Karl Popper there for the first time.
With the menace of the Nazis he was shortly to leave Vienna for
New Zealand, from which he eventually made his way to the
London School of Economics. An even more vivid memory is that of
my introducing Neurath to the noble but formidable Susan Stebbing
and his disconcerting her with the remark: 'I have always been for
the womans.' By that time Neurath was living in Holland. There
had been civil war in Vienna in 1934 when Dollfuss's right-wing
forces overthrew the Socialist municipal government and stormed
the Socialist stronghold, the Karl Marx Hof. Neurath was on their
list of wanted men but luckily he was in Moscow, on some business
connected with his Institute, which he then set up at The Hague.
Most of its work then consisted in the production of what he called
Isotypes, pictorial statistics.

If Neurath's removal weakened the Circle, a mortal blow was dealt
to it in 1936 by Moritz Schlick's murder. It was not a political act,
but the work of a demented former pupil. The right-wing press duly
deplored it, but there was a faint suggestion that this was the sort of
fate that radically anti-clerical professors might expect to suffer.

Neurath made a valiant attempt to keep the movement going. His
main ambition was to produce an International Encyclopaedia of
Unified Science, and he visited Chicago in 1936 to arrange for its
publication by the University Press. An organizing committee was
set up, consisting of himself, Carnap, Philipp Frank, Charles
Morris, who was teaching at Chicago, the Danish philosopher
Jørgen Jørgensen, whom the war was to turn into an ardent Marxist,
and Louis Rougier, pretty well the only French neo-positivist of the
time, who was to become an emissary of the Vichy government. The
encyclopaedia ran to nineteen monographs for the most part not
very distinguished with the notable exceptions of Carnap's *Logical
Foundations of the Unity of Science* and Ernest Nagel's *Principles of the
Theory of Probability*.

The German occupation of Austria dispersed the Circle. So far as
I know, only Neurath, Feigl, and Waismann among its members
were Jewish but the radical spirit of the group, and its rational

outlook, made it unacceptable to the Nazis. Vienna's loss was America's gain: Carnap holding a professorship first at Chicago and then in California. Frank, going to Harvard, Menger to Notre Dame, Gödel, perhaps the most gifted of them all, to the Institute at Princeton. I have said nothing about Gödel because his work lay wholly in the technical field of mathematical logic, and I doubt if even in his youth he wholeheartedly subscribed to the main doctrines of the Circle. As early as 1940, if Russell's evidence is to be trusted, his view of mathematics was Platonistic. Except for Kurt Grelling the Berlin group also escaped: Reichenbach and von Mises to California, after a stay in Istanbul, and Hempel early on to Brussels, and then to the United States, eventually establishing himself at Princeton. Of the Poles who survived the war, Kotarbinski and Ajdukiewicz remained in Poland, Łukasicwicz was sheltered by his pupil Scholz at Münster and subsequently became a professor in Dublin, and Tarski settled in California.

Even after 1938 Neurath tried to keep things going. He took over *Erkenntnis*, renamed it *The Journal of Unified Science* and arranged for it to be published at The Hague, but only a few numbers appeared. A final congress which I attended was held in Cambridge in 1938 but the only members of the Circle to come to it, besides Neurath and Waismann, were Frank and Feigl who came over from the United States. In 1940, when the Germans invaded Holland, Neurath and his third wife escaped to England as passengers on a crowded small boat. He was interned for some months as an enemy alien, and when released reopened his Institute. He died suddenly in December 1945, his last years having been devoted almost entirely to the production of his pictorial statistics. The other members of the Circle continued working but no longer as a group. Carnap was the most productive, his later work consisting almost entirely of an attempt to develop a system of inductive logic.

Von Juhos and Kraft remained in Vienna, inconspicuously, throughout the war, but the climate had changed, metaphysics was back* in fashion, and so far as the University of Vienna was concerned, the Circle might never have existed. It was different elsewhere. True, with the possible exception of myself, no one any longer cares to be called a logical positivist, but the Circle has left its imprint on successive generations of English philosophers, including Ryle and Austin and their disciples, on the work of Ernest Nagel, Quine, Nelson Goodman, Hilary Putnam, and other distinguished

American philosophers, on von Wright and Hintikka in Finland, on groups in Sweden and the Low Countries. Its influence has percolated even to Germany and France. If one goes through the theses advanced in the early numbers of *Erkenntnis* in detail one finds that nearly all of them are questionable and many of them false. But their spirit still triumphs. A strain of what I can best describe as woolly uplift was banished from philosophy – I daren't say never to return, that would be too optimistic – but where it survives or reappears, it has at least to face criticism of a keenness which we owe very largely to those heroes of my youth.